Christianity and the World

Essays Philosophical, Historical and Cultural

Jack Kerwick

Christianity and the World: Essays Philosophical, Historical and Cultural

Other books by Jack Kerwick
The American Offensive: Dispatches from the Front
Misguided Guardians: The Conservative Case against Neoconservatism

© 2017 Jack Kerwick All Rights Reserved
Print ISBN 978-1-941071-75-5
ebook ISBN 978-1-941071-76-2

This book is sold subject to the condition that it shall not, by way of trade or otherwise, be lent, resold, hired out or otherwise circulated without the publisher's prior consent in any form of binding or cover other than that in which it is published and without a similar condition including this condition being imposed on the subsequent purchaser.

STAIRWAY PRESS—APACHE JUNCTION

Cover Design by Guy D. Corp
www.GrafixCorp.com

STAIRWAY≡PRESS

www.StairwayPress.com
1000 West Apache Trail #126
Apache Junction, AZ 88120 USA

INTRODUCTION

LAST YEAR, DURING a faculty conversation at the college at which I teach philosophy, a colleague, who is also a friend, posed a question regarding a very specific set of circumstances that had her troubled: Ours is a secular institution and yet the Gideons, members of an evangelical Christian organization, gathered on campus to distribute pocket sized copies of the Bible to students, faculty, and staff alike.

"Why do they do that?" she asked. Her question was obviously rhetorical—she didn't think that the Gideons should have been engaged in the activity of disseminating religious literature to strangers, but particularly strangers in a non-religious, or at least non-Christian, location.

Yet it was equally obvious to me that her question wasn't *only* rhetorical. My friend sincerely, genuinely didn't understand the Gideons' evangelism.

She didn't know that the Gideons distribute Bibles because they believe that it is their calling as Christians to make disciples of all nations, to preach the Gospel to the four corners of the world.

Not being a Christian herself, my colleague and friend could not have recognized that in asking about *those Gideons* who were handing out *those Bibles* to students on *this campus*, she pointed to a much more fundamental question.

She was essentially asking a question concerning Christianity itself.

Why do Christians do what they do? *Why do they do that?*

This inquiry of my friend's proved to be the final catalyst for the composition of this book.

It was not, however, the only impetus. Illiteracy regarding Christianity is hardly limited to non-Christians. It is endemic throughout our culture. This mass ignorance is made that much more painful by the fact that, for the better part of the last two millennia, the collective consciousness of what is today known as Western civilization or "the West," i.e. European civilization, has been informed by the religion of Christianity.

Thus, for no small measure of this time, the West was known by its own inhabitants and others simply as "Christendom."

Indeed, there is scarcely any aspect of our world, however unremarkable and mundane, that doesn't bear the impress of its Christian pedigree. Scandalously, an ever-increasing number of Westerners, both Christian and non-Christian alike, seem unaware of this fact. Those who aren't oblivious to their Christian inheritance are hostile to it. Yet they too are ignorant, for their antagonism toward it renders them blind to the debt owed by their own secular ideologies to the tradition that they despise.

This book is intended as an antidote of sorts to the present condition. It is not meant to be read as an introduction to all things Christian, the equivalent of a "Christianity for Dummies" or "Christianity made simple." Nor is it a work of theology or Biblical exegesis.

This book targets an intellectually curious lay audience, it's true. Its aim is to increase the reader's understanding of Christianity by focusing on a select range of topics that, collectively, will deliver both theoretical and practical enlightenment, a knowledge of Christian theism considered as a philosophy as well as an awareness of the ways in which Christianity has impacted, continues to impact, and is impacted by the world.

The first chapter identifies the comprehensive range of respects in which Christianity has fundamentally transformed the world. Scientifically, morally, politically, aesthetically, theologically, philosophically—in every conceivable way, Christianity revolutionized our world. As I write in *Christianity and the Transformation of History*, Christianity didn't *change* history. It *became* history.

In Chapter II, *Christianity and Morality: The Atheist's Problem of Moral Goodness*, I restate and refute the arguments made by such "new" atheists as Sam Harris that morality can remain objective in the absence of God.

What's traditionally been known as "the problem of evil" is the theist's philosophical or theological challenge of reconciling his belief in an omnipotent and all-good God with the presence of evil in the world. Here, I show that those atheists like Harris, who want to preserve an essentially theistic, specifically Christian, conception of morality while jettisoning theism and Christianity are saddled with just the opposite problem, what I refer to in the title as "the problem of goodness." This is the problem of reconciling their belief in a purely material, meaningless cosmos with the objectivity of moral (and other sorts of) value.

The Rational Defensibility of Christian Theism and the Atheist's Weak Case Against It is the third chapter. It's a common misconception that Christianity has nothing behind it but "blind faith," a faith entirely divorced from reason. The reality, however, is that some of the brightest thinkers that have ever lived, over a span of many centuries, expended incredible intellectual energy into revealing the mutually supportive relationship between reason and faith. Several arguments or "proofs" for God's existence were devised and revised to meet criticisms.

Many of these arguments retain their defenders to this day.

Here, I introduce readers to some of them. I also look specifically at the objections leveled against them by prominent "new atheist" and biologist, Richard Dawkins. These objections are representative of much contemporary thought in being thought*less*: they reflect at once gross misunderstanding of their targets and shoddy thinking on their own terms.

The title of the fourth chapter, *Christianity: The Most Persecuted of Religions*, is self-explanatory. There is much talk today about so-called "Islamophobia," to say nothing of discrimination *by Christians* against numerous other groups. The truth, however, is that there is no religious group in the world that is more persecuted than that of Christianity.

Through a number of short essays, the reader will become acquainted with this cancerous phenomenon, what some have called "*Christophobia.*"

The fifth and final chapter, *Christianity and Culture* consists of shorter essays on the many ways in which Christianity continues to interact with the dominant Western, specifically American, culture. Issues like abortion, "gay marriage," and several others are here addressed.

Regardless of the order in which the installments in this book are read—and they can be read in any order—the engaged reader promises to realize the endgame of a more informed perspective of the Christian tradition. It is my hope that upon completion of this work, the reader will be in a better position to answer my colleague's inquiry:

"Why do they do that?"

CHAPTER I

Christianity and the Transformation of History

HIS 2 BILLION or so disciples today are of one mind with the countless millions of their counterparts from over the last two millennia that have recognized in the Carpenter from Galilee the Author of the universe.

Jesus of Nazareth, Christians have always believed, is the Son of God, or God the Son, the Second Person of the Triune God made flesh. Christmas is the celebration of this event, the moment when the Son of God enters the world as a babe in a manger. This is what Christians recognize as "the Incarnation." Easter is the commemoration of how God, through His glorious Passion, Death, and Resurrection from the dead, rescues humanity from its sinful condition and reconciles it with its divine Author.

Yet one needn't accept the deity of Jesus or, for that matter, any deity whatsoever in order to grant that, unquestionably, no one who has ever lived has impacted the course of human history to the extent to which Jesus of Nazareth has impacted it. In fact, to speak this way is to dramatically understate matters, for such was the power of His life that Jesus didn't just *impact* history; He radically *subverted* it.

To put it even more accurately, history, as we know it, has been Christianized.

Jesus was in history. By the time that his short 33 years on Earth came to a close, history would be in Him. The world today measures time and history ("B.C." and "A.D.") around the life of this man. As the Reverend D. James Kennedy puts it, "Jesus Christ, the greatest man who ever lived, has changed virtually every aspect of human life [.]" Kennedy informs us that "its humble origins" aside, "the Church has made more changes on earth for the good than any other movement or force in history." [1] Indeed.

Women

Today, in the West, it is taken for granted that women, though different from men, are moral equals with the latter.

This, like virtually every other aspect of the moral sense that continues to inform the consciousness of Western peoples, is a legacy of Christianity.

It isn't just that in the ancient Greco-Roman world, the setting within which Christianity initially emerged, women were assigned a role subordinate to that assigned to men. Women were perceived as being of lesser value than men. This accounts for why female infants were frequently either killed or abandoned to die, and it explains why Roman and Greek men held marriage generally and their wives specifically in low esteem.

Rodney Stark, the eminent sociologist of religion, writes: "Exposure of unwanted female infants and deformed male infants was legal, morally accepted, and widely practiced by all social classes in the Greco-Roman world." Alluding to a study of inscriptions in the Greek city of Delphi, Stark notes that its findings reveal that a mere six of 600 families reared more than one daughter.[2] He also refers to a particularly telling letter from a Greek man to his pregnant wife in which the former implores the latter to "take good care of our baby son" until he returns home. The man is equally insistent that if his wife is "delivered of a child," and "if it is a boy," then she is to "keep it [.]" However, if it is a girl, he continues, "discard it."[3]

Because of the prevalence of infanticide and abortion, a substantial gender imbalance between males and females emerged throughout the Roman Empire. In Italy, Asia Minor, and North Africa, there were as many as 140 males for every 100 females.[4]

Things were not much different in Athens. As Stark writes, "The status of Athenian women was very low." He elaborates:

> *Girls received little or no education. Typically, Athenian females were married at puberty and often before. Under Athenian law a woman was classified as a child, regardless of age, and therefore was the legal property of some man at all stages of in her life. Males could divorce by simply ordering a wife out of the household. Moreover, if a woman was seduced or raped, her husband was legally compelled to divorce her. If a woman wanted a divorce, she had to have her father or some other man bring her case before a judge. Finally, Athenian women could own property, but control of the property was always vested in the male to whom she 'belonged.'*[5]

Things were otherwise for women in the world that the Christians created. The Christian attitudes toward both marriage and human life as a whole both gave rise to and reflected the elevation of women from the status that they assumed in the ancient world.

That Christianity proscribed abortion and infanticide for *all* human beings certainly explains the precipitously lower female mortality rate that existed in the pagan world. Its transformation of marriage into a sacrament, though, supplies history with the most resounding affirmation of the moral equality of men and women that had yet to have been provided.

Jesus's monogamous ideal—*So they are no longer two, but one flesh*—was read as implying a proscription of divorce and marital infidelity. In glaring contrast to the gender practices of their pagan counterparts, by the lights of Christianity, it wasn't just women who were expected to be chaste until marriage. All forms of extramarital and/or non-marital sexual activity were condemned as adulterous.[6]

Widows too benefited greatly from Christianity. In the classical world widows faced harsh legal and social sanctions if they waited more than a couple of years to remarry. If a widow was wealthy, her resources would come under the ownership of her new husband. Christians, though, respected widowhood. And they didn't just talk the talk: Affluent widows were permitted to keep their inheritances while the church community took care of those who were of more modest means.[7]

Anthony Esolen summarizes the Christian view of women. Christians, he tells us, "did not expose baby girls (or boys, either). They did not divorce their wives. They shunned sexual practices that put them and their spouses at risk. They honored women who defied emperors, centurions and soldiers to witness to the faith."[8]

The earliest Christian church consisted of as many, if not slightly more, women than it did men, a fact that earned for it the contempt of Romans who regarded it as "a religion for women."[9]

Children

Of course, it is not just women whose lot in the world had been immeasurably improved courtesy of the emergence of

Christianity and the World

Christianity. So too had that of children been elevated. While it was especially common for ancients to abandon and/or directly kill female infants, male children, specifically those who were born with deformities of one sort or other, were also frequently left to die. And those children who made it beyond infancy remained wholly at the mercies of their parents.

In Rome, for instance, the *paterfamilias*, the father of the household, possessed near total authority over the life and limb of the members of his family. At one juncture, it was lawful for him to even kill his children. The annals of Roman history contain stories of men like Torquatus ("The Man with the Neck Chain") and Lucius Junius Brutus, men who ordered the deaths of their adult sons who defied orders in battle and who were regarded as heroes.[10]

The parent-child relationship was conceived quite differently within the Christian vision. The world's first orphanages, nurseries, and foundling homes arose courtesy of Christians. From its inception, Christianity forbade child abandonment, infanticide, and abortion. It even proscribed birth control. Christians saw themselves as commissioned to attend to the poor and the needy—irrespectively of age.

In the medieval era, every parish town eventually had a set of arrangements that made provisions for orphans, and in 18th century England, a devout, seafaring Christian philanthropist by the name of Thomas Coram established the first foundling hospital, a home devised for the purpose of the "education and maintenance of exposed and deserted children."[11] It was also during the 18th century that Ursuline nuns founded the first "orphan asylum" in North America.[12]

That children—*all* children—are entitled to an education is also an idea unique to Christianity. In the United States, for example, Catholic nuns have rightly been recognized as "pioneers" in education and "the country's first professional elementary school teachers,"[13] and the Framers of the Constitution were unequivocal in expressing their belief that elementary schools were needed to supply to children an education in the Christian prerequisites for ordered liberty.[14]

Charity

Charity, which Westerners have long taken for granted as a moral imperative, is not unique to Christianity. However, as the Jewish writer Ilana Mercer notes, it was most definitely "perfected" by the latter.[15]

D. James Kennedy observes that prior to Christianity, the world "was like the Russian tundra—quite cold and inhospitable." He notes that exhaustive research of the historical record can only lead us to conclude that no "organized charitable effort" had ever existed in antiquity before the rise of Christianity. Thus, prior to Christianity and the Bible that it sought to export to the four corners of the globe, "Disinterested benevolence was unknown." Posterior to Christianity, though, "charity and benevolence flourished."[16]

How true. The Salvation Army; Samaritan's Purse; World Vision; Catholic Charities; the Red Cross; Catholic Relief Services; Christian Foundation for Children and Aging; and Operation Blessing are among the innumerable charitable organizations that Christianity has bequeathed to the world. Each and every church—not denomination, mind you, but each and every individual congregation—that exists has multiple ministries aimed at alleviating the plight of the poor and needy.

That scores of Western secularists have created charitable organizations only underscores the extent to which they've appropriated the legacy of the very religion that they reject. Scholar Anthony Esolen reminds them that "charity and concern for the poor are integral to our culture today *because* of Christianity." Elaborating, he writes:

Christianity and the World

> *If we build hospitals for the destitute beyond our own lands, with no desire for personal or national profit, and risking life and limb to do it, it is because we retain a trace, a cultural memory of the voyages of [such Christian heroes as] Saint Paul, of Boniface martyred by the Germans, of Cyril and Methodius trekking north among the Slavs, of Patrick driving the snakes from Ireland, of Gregory the Great seeing blond slaves in the marketplace and, hearing that they were called "Angli," replying,…"not Angles but angels," and sending missionaries among them, to give them the best he had to give.*

While noting that it may not be "polite to say so," Esolen underscores the uniquely Christian character of the culture of charity that has emerged in the West by distinguishing it from those cultures produced by other religious and philosophical traditions.[17] Hindus, Buddhists, Muslims and the adherents of Shinto—none of them dispatch missionaries throughout the world to feed the hungry and clothe the naked.

Hindus do very little to attend to the needs and wants of the inhabitants of their own lands who occupy the lowest rungs or "castes" in the social order. Doubtless, this is due to the Hindu metaphysic, the notion that, ultimately, the individual or ego is a toxic illusion that fuels the potentially endless series of birth, death, and rebirth, i.e. reincarnation. On this cyclical conception of reality, the objective is for "the individual" to achieve emancipation from this rollercoaster by recognizing that he or she isn't a distinct individual at all but of the same substance or being as God. If the individual doesn't ultimately exist and the world of sensible things that we take for reality is just a dreamy, a nightmarish, appearance that arises from the egocentric fiction of the self, then why expend precious time and resources fortifying the dream by forsaking precious resources to make the world better? The world, or at least what we assume is the world, is not real.

Buddhism proceeds from the same cyclical vision of reality affirmed by the Hinduism from which it spun off. Only here, it is "Nirvana" that is or should be the aim of human activity. Nirvana is a transcendent state in which the illusory sense of a self or soul is not absorbed into God, as in Hinduism, but extinguished altogether. As the means to this end, Buddhists demand *detachment* from the world.

The cultural-specificity of Shinto and even Confucianism precludes the universal or trans-cultural vocation to which Christians are called. As for Islam, while its followers insist at least as much as Christians upon the distinction between Creator and creation, that Muslims do not deploy missionaries to the ends of the Earth to minister to strangers in need may have something to do with their belief that the Quran is God incarnate and the Quran commands Muslims to care for fellow Muslims. Even Judaism, from which Christianity arose, was anchored in a specific people and bore the unmistakable impress of its culture.

Matters are otherwise with Christianity. "The preciousness and equal moral worth of every human life is a Christian idea," Dinesh D'Souza writes in *What's So Great About Christianity?*

> *Christians have always believed that God places infinite value on each human life He creates and that He loves each person equally.*

Unlike in other religious traditions, like even Judaism, in Christianity "you are not saved through your family or tribe or city. Salvation is an individual matter."[18] Christianity alone "cultivated an appreciation for individuality."[19] Its universality and individuality combined to give rise to the uniquely Christian understanding of compassion for all as a moral mandate.

The modern hospital has its roots in Christianity. While homes and centers designed to care for the sick existed in some places in the ancient world, it was only after Christianity became the religion of the Roman Empire that we witness the exponential expansion of this phenomenon. The Christian origins of the modern hospital are unmistakable.

In the fourth century, a hospital would be built in every cathedral town.[20] These hospitals would attend to various classes of patients, offer training programs for those entering the field of medicine, and maintain libraries where physicians would conduct medical and pharmacological research. Albert Jonsen[21] a historian of medicine, credits Christianity with what he describes as "the second great sweep of medical history," a 1,000 year reign beginning at the end of the fourth century and lasting until the end of the 14th century when "medicine [was] well ensconced in the universities and in the public life of the emerging nations of Europe."[22] Others too have meticulously traced the Christian pedigree of the modern hospital.[23]

While the first hospitals were initially built by Christians for Christians, soon they would be made available to all, including, remarkably, Muslims who were only in Christian lands because they invaded them for purposes of conquest.[24]

Education

Christianity has spearheaded the movement to educate the masses. Kennedy states:

> *Every school you see—public or private, religious or secular—is a visible reminder of the religion of Jesus Christ. So is every college and university[.]*

The truth "is that the phenomenon of education for the masses has its roots in Christianity. Christianity gave rise to the concept of education for everyone." [25]

Institutions of higher learning were Christian in conception. Of the 123 colleges that we find at America's origins, all but one had an explicitly Christian mission. Princeton, Harvard, and Yale, to name three prominent examples, were Christian. England's Oxford and Cambridge Universities were also Christian, as was St. Andrew's, Scotland's oldest university.

When, in the 12th century, medieval Christendom gave rise to the university, it introduced to the world a phenomenon the likes of which had never been seen before. Unlike those educational institutions that existed in the East, in places like China, say, and unlike even those that existed among the Greeks and Romans, academies that were more interested in *imparting* what had been inherited, universities existed for the sake of *pursuing* knowledge. It was within these medieval universities, presided over by faculty that were members of religious orders, that science took flight.[26]

The Arts

Whether it was literature, architecture, sculpture, painting, or music, Christians all but revolutionized the arts.

Medieval Christians pioneered not only vernacular prose insofar as they wrote in the tongues of their native lands, rather than in Latin, but the flying buttress, an achievement that rendered it possible to construct high buildings with large windows. This achievement in turn spawned subsequent successes with stained glass.

The medieval era as well gave rise to the use of oil painting and the stretched canvas (as opposed to wood or plaster) that made it possible for "the painter to take his time, to use brushes of amazing delicacy, to achieve effects...which seemed close to miracles." [27]

In music, Christians advanced over the ancients in producing polyphonies, i.e. harmonies.[28] They as well developed and promoted a system of musical notation that allowed for musicians who had never heard a piece of music to nevertheless perform it.

Consider, had Christ never lived, there never would have existed Michelangelo, Da Vinci, Dante, Chaucer, Shakespeare, Handel, and Bach, to name but a handful of history's most renowned artists. Nor, for that matter, would we have ever heard of the likes of William Wordsworth and Samuel Taylor Coleridge, writers who, though not explicitly Christian, traded in Christian themes, to say nothing of those like George Elliot and Thomas Harding whose "mode of criticism" of Christianity "often reflects a subtle appropriation, development, or modification of Christian assumptions."[29]

Slavery

Slavery is an institution that has been practiced for as long as there had been human beings.

Though one wouldn't know it from the racial politics of contemporary Western societies and America especially, there is scarcely an ethnic, racial, and/or religious group that hasn't at some point assumed the roles of *both* enslaved and enslaver.

Moralists and the pious alike had accepted slavery as an unquestioned feature of human existence. Some, like Aristotle, defended the arrangement of human bondage as "natural" and, thus, morally unobjectionable. Muhammad, the Prophet of Islam, owned slaves.

None of this, of course, means that anyone looked forward to becoming another's slave: Slave revolts of various sorts occurred for thousands of years. However, the resistance with which slavery was met by the enslaved no more reflected respect for moral principle on the part of the latter than does the resistance of a gazelle to a lion reflect the gazelle's commitment to a principle enjoining lions to refrain from consuming mammals. That *I* do not want to be enslaved does not mean that I recognize the *wrongness* of slavery *per se*. Plato, for example, opposed the enslavement of his fellow Greeks, but even the ideal state that he envisioned required the enslavement of barbarians (non-Greeks). And, in point of fact, there were no abolitionist movements or literature anywhere in the world—until the advent of Christianity.

It was within Christian culture that the moral character of slavery first came into question. Remarkably, centuries before the modern world treated as an axiom the wrongness of slavery, this perennial practice was banned throughout Christendom. Opposition to slavery began to show as early as the 600's. In the eighth century, Charlemagne, the Holy Roman Emperor, joined with the Pope and the leadership of the Church to expressly condemn it, and by the ninth century, it was widely accepted that "slavery in itself was against divine law."[30]

Of course, the worldwide ban on slavery didn't occur until many centuries after the Middle Ages had retreated into history. Still, it is undeniable that the impulse to eradicate slavery from the face of the Earth was fundamentally religious, specifically and unmistakably Christian.

It was in the 18th century, at the apex of the British Empire, that devout Christians represented by the likes of William Wilberforce spearheaded the movement to stamp out slavery wherever the Empire's influence extended. Upon his conversion to Christianity, Wilberforce wrote in his diary in 1787 that God was calling him to work toward the suppression of the slave trade. By the 1830's, with the Slavery Abolition Act of 1833, slavery had been abolished.[31]

Courtesy of its immense military, economic, and political resources, the British eventually succeeded in coercing other peoples, particularly Africans, Asians, and Arabs who didn't relent easily, to abandon slavery.[32]

That Christian civilization was the only in the world to recognize in slavery an affront against the dignity of the individual is unsurprising given that this civilization is unique in resoundingly affirming the inviolable dignity, the glory, of *the individual*. As Rodney Stark characterizes it, "the Western sense of individualism was largely a Christian creation."[33] The point is well taken. While individuality, understood in some sense of this term, emerged episodically and in degrees in other time and places[34] it wasn't until Christianity arose that it came unapologetically into its own. Christianity supplied three things that, conjointly, elevated the individual to a level of distinction that remains historically unprecedented.

First, Christianity advanced a doctrine of universal salvation. Unlike most other religious and philosophical traditions that endowed with significance some set or other of contingent factors—class, culture, ethnicity, etc.—that differentiated the enlightened from the unenlightened, Christianity promised salvation to, not *a* people, and not even all *peoples,* but *all people*. Every single *person,* it declares, can avail themselves of the gift of salvation.

Second, the salvation that Christianity proclaims *is* a *gift*. Unlike, say, Buddhism, which expects for each person to "*work*" out his or her own salvation "with diligence," Christianity insists that salvation is a gift, a priceless gift that has been freely and graciously given by a loving Creator-God who created humanity in His image. Thus, this gift is offered to every human being.

Thirdly, Christianity insists upon the doctrine of free will. Until Judaism introduced monotheism, the world's religions and philosophies essentially shared the same metaphysic: The universe was not only without beginning or end, it was cyclical in nature. This conception of the cosmos, with its fatalistic implications, left little to no room for the notion of free will.

However, once it was accepted that the universe did indeed come into being at some finite time through the agency of an infinite, personal God, and once it was accepted that time and history move, not cyclically, but in a linear progression, the belief in free will became inescapable.

Since God is not just the supreme Being, but supremely personal, the Creator, Conserver, and Redeemer of the human race who, as such, has expectations of those of His creatures who He made after His likeness, humans must have the freedom to either accept God's invitation to be stewards of His creation or reject it. Though it accepted these suppositions, Judaism's primary focus nevertheless fastened upon the experiences and aspirations of a culturally and ethnically-specific collectivity, a people. The universality and inclusiveness of the Christian vision, though, emancipated the individual from all contingencies of time and place.

America

The United States of America itself would be unthinkable in the absence of Christianity. For starters, and most obviously, those who settled the country, its founding stock, were, well, Christian: Many were practicing Christians and even those who weren't had been reared within the Christian tradition. There is no getting around this brute, demographical fact. And—shocker of shockers—the ideas that comprised their collective religious consciousness actually informed their plans for the society that they were forming. Though it should go without saying, the prevailing secular zeitgeist of the last century as well as our own requires, unfortunately, that we remind ourselves of this. This brings us to the next point.

While it is doubtless true that America is the product of the Enlightenment, it is no less true that many of the ideas, principles,

Christianity and the World

and images that saturate the Founding are unmistakably those that we'd expect to find from *Protestant Christians*.

Actually, and contrary to what contemporary secular historians would have us think, the Biblical influence was significantly stronger upon the Founders than that of such philosophers as John Locke. Michael Novak writes: "Before Locke was even born, the Pilgrims believed in the consent of the governed, social compacts, the dignity of every child of God, and political equality." [35]

In other words, prior to the works of those modern or Enlightenment thinkers, like Locke, which are customarily cited as the biggest influences on the men who fashioned the country, "Americans had fashioned a political doctrine from the Hebrew Bible, and had acquired historically unparalleled practice in the arts of self-government." [36]

Novak refers to "the Hebrew metaphysic," the metaphysic that Christians exported to the world and that underwrites the American experiment. This involves "a narrative of purpose and progress."

Unlike virtually all non-Jewish, pre-Christian cultures, those who endorsed this Hebrew metaphysic rejected the notion that "time is cyclical, going nowhere, spinning in circles pointlessly." Rather, they held that "history had a *beginning* and was guided by Providence for a *purpose*." [37]

"Time," the Founders maintained, "was created for the *unfolding of human liberty,* for human emancipation" and history "is a record of progress (or decline), measured by permanent standards, God's standards, as learned from and tested by long experience." [38]

Novak explains that history so understood—"open, purposive, contingent in liberty"—is unique to Judaism and Christianity. "Probably most of the humans who had ever lived before the arrival of Judaism on the world stage never even heard of 'progress.'" Greeks and Romans were representative of much of the ancient world inasmuch as they tended to look to past golden ages. For Jews and Christians, though, "history is heading somewhere new: toward the New Kingdom of God, a kingdom of justice and love and peace, a new city on a hill." [39]

And this new city on a hill earlier generations of Americans equated with the new country that they were busy fashioning.

Science

Christianity gave rise to modern science. Science depends upon certain non-scientific suppositions regarding the nature of reality in the absence of which it never would've arisen.

That the world is real; that it is rational or orderly, governed by natural laws that render it *capable* of being explored and discovered; and that it is good, *deserving* of being studied—are assumptions that are thoroughly Christian in character.

It is not by accident that the first and greatest of scientists—Galileo, Roger Bacon, Copernicus, Kepler, Pascal, Newton, Boyle, and Mendel, to name but a few—were Bible-believing Christians. Rodney Stark, distinguished sociologist of religion, makes the relevant point: "Not only were science and religion compatible, they were inseparable—the rise of science was achieved by deeply religious Christian scholars." [40] This will doubtless come as an enormous shock to such Christophobic atheists as Richard Dawkins, Sam Harris, and their ilk. Yet it is true all of the same.

In his introduction, Stark cuts to the quick in identifying why all too few Westerners are aware of the richness of their religious inheritance. "During the past century, Western intellectuals have been more willing to trace European imperialism to Christian origins, but they have been entirely unwilling to recognize that Christianity made any contribution (other than intolerance) to the Western capacity to dominate."

Instead, "the West is said to have surged ahead precisely as it *overcame* religious barriers to progress, especially those impeding science."[41]

It is the desire to perpetuate this narrative that accounts for why its purveyors depict the era of what is now recognized as the Scientific Revolution as the historical moment when science spontaneously erupted from the morass of religious superstition and myth. The only problem with this conventional wisdom is that it is itself on the order of superstition and myth.[42]

Stark's reply to this conventional wisdom is to the point: "Nonsense." He is unequivocal: "The success of the West, including the rise of science, rested *entirely* on religious foundations, and the people who brought it about were devout Christians."[43]

The emergence of modern science was the culmination of centuries' worth of the achievements of medieval Christian thinkers. Specifically, science was made possible by the twelfth-century creation of the university—another of Christianity's gifts to humanity. The belief in the rationality of the material world is nothing more or less than a belief that the universe is governed by natural laws. In the absence of this idea, science never could have come about.

Stark draws our attention to the common error of confusing technology and observation with science. "Science," he writes, "is a *method* utilized in *organized* efforts to formulate *explanations of nature,* always subject to modifications and corrections through *systematic observations.*" What this means is that science consists of two parts: theory and research.[44] "Hence, the earlier technical innovations of Greco-Roman times, of Islam, of China, let alone those achieved in pre-historical times, do not constitute science and are better described as lore, skills, wisdom, techniques, crafts, technologies, engineering, learning, or simply knowledge."[45]

Stark is blunt: "Real science arose only once: in Europe"—in *Christian* Europe. "China, Islam, India, and ancient Greece and Rome each had a highly developed alchemy. But only in Europe did alchemy develop into chemistry. By the same token, many societies developed elaborate systems of astrology, but only in Europe did astrology develop into astronomy." [46]

The reason for this has everything to do with Christian Europe's vision of God.

To further substantiate his point, Stark quotes Alfred North Whitehead, a 20th century philosopher and mathematician who co-authored, with the famed atheist philosopher, Bertrand Russell, their *Principia Mathematica*. While delivering a Lowell Lecture at Harvard in the 1920's, Whitehead shocked his fellow academics when he remarked that "faith in the possibility of science" derived from "medieval theology."

Whitehead elaborated: "The greatest contribution of medievalism to the formation of the scientific movement," he remarked, was "the inexpugnable belief" in "a secret that can be unveiled." That this "conviction" has seized "the European mind" can only be explained in terms of "the medieval insistence on the rationality of God, conceived as with the personal energy of Jehovah and with the rationality of a Greek philosopher." This conception of God led to the notion that every "detail" in nature "was supervised and ordered: the search into nature could only result in the vindication of the faith in rationality." [47]

And there is no question that all of the great scientists of the early modern era, men like Descartes, Galileo, Newton, and Kepler, "confess[ed]...their absolute faith in a creator God, whose work incorporated rational rules awaiting discovery." [48]

In summary, Stark writes that far from being "an extension of classical learning," the emergence of science "was the natural outgrowth of Christian doctrine," a doctrine that attributes nature's existence to a creative act on the part of God. Moreover, the "love and honor" of God require that we "fully appreciate the wonders of his handiwork. Because God is perfect, his handiwork functions in accord with *immutable principles*. By the full use of our God-given powers of reason and observation, it ought to be possible to discover these principles."

He concludes: "These were the crucial ideas that explain why science arose in Christian Europe and nowhere else." [49]

The Rise of "Capitalism"

It was this emergence of the individual to which Christianity gave rise that led not only to the belief in moral equality and the abolition of slavery but, as well, the rise of "capitalism."

The technological innovations that Christians made possible facilitated the development of capitalism, but the individual is the moral-ontological presupposition of this system. Before proceeding, however, we should define this term that, after all, was first coined by its enemies.

Stark's definition of what is now regarded as "capitalism" is the best available. "Capitalism," he writes:

> *is an economic system wherein privately owned, relatively well organized, and stable firms pursue complex commercial activities within a relatively free (unregulated) market, taking a systematic, long-term approach to investing and reinvesting wealth (directly or indirectly) in productive activities involving a hired workforce, and guided by anticipated and actual returns.* [50]

Capitalism, so understood, consists in a banking system, credit, diversification, minimal immediate producer-to-consumer interactions, and so forth. And it presupposes virtues like honesty, diligence, deferred gratification, and the like.

Monastic orders owned the great estates of medieval Christendom. During the 800's, the monastics began specializing in the cultivation of specific kinds of crops which they then sold for a profit. In using the proceeds to satisfy their other needs, they in turn ushered in a cash economy. They also reinvested these profits in their daily enterprises, a move that vastly increased their revenues and which ultimately enabled them to become banks, lending institutions whose customers were members of the nobility.[51]

Over time, as gains in productivity became more rapid and substantial, areas of specialization and trade both took flight.

Belief in the inviolable dignity of the individual produced the notion that labor is *dignified*. Stark notes that pre-Christian societies "celebrate[d] consumption" while disdaining work. "Notions such as the dignity of labor or the idea that work is a virtuous activity," he continues, "were incomprehensible in ancient Rome or in any other precapitalist society. Rather, just as spending is the purpose of wealth, the preferred approach to work is to have someone else do it and, failing that, to do as little as possible."[52]

Capitalist societies, in marked contrast, hold an entirely different perspective, with work regarded as "intrinsically virtuous [.]" Moreover, self-restraint in consumption is also viewed as a character excellence.

Long after the medieval era had passed, Max Weber characterized this orientation as "the *Protestant* ethic," the implication being that it was a post-Catholic and modern phenomenon. Yet centuries earlier, as we have seen, Catholic monks and nuns exemplified these virtues in their daily lives while developing that intricate, revolutionary, life-enriching economic system that we today call "capitalism."[53]

Conclusion

Indeed, in every conceivable way the world that contemporary Westerners, both secular and religious, Christian and non-Christian alike, take for granted would never have come to be had it not been for the Carpenter from Galilee and His disciples.

Scientifically, technologically, aesthetically, politically, and morally—that which has made the West a magnet for the rest of the planet and which has immeasurably improved beyond the wildest dreams of peoples from other times and places the quality of life for untold millions and even billions of human beings is an enduring legacy of Christianity.

As cultural commentator, journalist, and atheist Fred Reed notes, efforts on the part of contemporary secularists to "dismiss Christianity as crude superstition" are "unfortunate," "stupid," and reflect a profound "historical illiteracy," for Christianity "was the heart and soul of as yet the greatest civilization the world has seen." Since it "shaped the culture, art, philosophy, literature, the very framework of mind" of our world—most which "was superb and remains unsurpassed"—Reed remarks that those who are oblivious to this brute fact "cannot understand the last two thousand years and how our world came to be." [54]

For this reason alone, everyone should be grateful to Jesus—even if they don't accept that He was the Christ.

CHAPTER II

Christianity and Morality: The Atheist's Problem of Moral Goodness

SAM HARRIS, WHOSE Ph.D. is in cognitive neuroscience, is no fan of theism, whether Christian or otherwise. In this regard, he is no different from any number of other atheists. However, Harris's statement of atheism is not without distinction, for the reasoning upon which it depends—comprised as it is of non sequiturs, straw men, and ad hominem fallacies—is especially weak. Because of the bad faith in which he argues, because of the contempt and condescension that Harris has for his opponents, in an ideal world he would be met with the silence that he deserves. In the real world, though, a world in which Harris exerts a significant influence over many, his assertions cannot afford to go unaddressed, for in many ways they represent the shoddy thinking concerning religion that pervades the thought of untold numbers of religiously illiterate people.

In his *Letter to a Christian Nation,* Harris makes a number of claims against Christianity and theism that are as old and familiar as they are historically, theologically, and philosophically ignorant.

These charges essentially constitute the objection that Christianity, far from making the world a better place, actually makes it a worse place by facilitating suffering—which Harris equates with what in another idiom has been called "evil." In other words, the crux of Harris's critique is that Christianity is, ultimately, immoral.

Objective or Real Morality

Harris writes that Christians "believe that Christianity is an unrivaled source of human goodness," "that Jesus taught the virtues of love, compassion, and selflessness better than any teacher who has ever lived," and that the Bible, being "the most profound book ever written," "must have been divinely inspired."[1]

The problem with these beliefs, according to Harris, is that they are all "false." Yet they are not only false; they are patently false. "The idea that the Bible," Harris continues, "is a perfect guide to morality[,] is simply astounding, given the contents of the book."[2]

The problem with Christian or religious morality, as Harris sees it, is that it is actually immoral because Christians separate morality from "the reality of human and animal suffering."[3] Christians "believe that unless the Bible is accepted as the word of God, there can be no universal standard of morality. But we can easily think of objective sources of moral order that do not require the existence of a lawgiving God."

If, Harris continues, there are "better and worse ways to seek happiness in this world,"[4] if there are "psychological laws that govern human well-being, knowledge of these laws would provide an enduring basis for an objective morality."[5]

It is "an objective claim about the human mind, about the dynamics of social relations, and about the moral order of our world" that "love is more conducive to happiness than hate is."

Thus, happiness requires that we love others, and this, in turn, requires "self-sacrifice and self-denial."

The pursuit of one's happiness, in other words, will at times demand "enormous sacrifices for the good of others" that are "essential for one's own deeper well-being." [6]

Sounding essentially this same theme, Harris says elsewhere that we do not need the Ten Commandments in order to know that the activities that they proscribe are wrong. "It is a scientific fact that moral emotions—like a sense of fair play or an abhorrence of cruelty—precede exposure to scripture." In fact, science "reveals" that *animals* too are "generally intolerant of murder and theft," [7] "deception" and "sexual betrayal." [8]

There are several comments that are in order here.

First, though it is correct that Christians across denominations hold that the Bible consists of divinely-inspired Scriptures, Harris misconstrues the Christian's position. It is *not* the case that Christians maintain that in the absence of *the Bible* objective morality is impossible. Contrary to what Harris would have his readers believe, most Christians, like Jews before them, have always recognized that the Bible, while ethically illustrative, is neither necessary nor sufficient for either the existence of objective morality or our knowledge of it. Rather, like some illustrious atheist thinkers, Christians recognize that in the absence of *God,* the notion of objective moral truth becomes difficult to sustain.

Take, for example, the 19th century philosopher Friedrich Nietzsche, who famously (or infamously) announced that "God is dead." Nietzsche didn't, of course, mean to suggest that God had literally ceased to exist. He didn't believe that God was real. What Nietzsche meant was that the decline in *theistic belief,* specifically, Christian monotheism, that he saw spreading throughout Europe necessarily translated into a loss of the only justification for belief in objective morality that had been available for nearly two millennia.

Christianity and the World

Simply put, in denying God's existence, European peoples, whether they liked it or not, denied objective morality, for without a transcendent moral lawgiver, there is no universal, objective moral law. In divesting himself of his theism, European Man divested objective morality of its ground. This, Nietzsche insists, is a good thing, for it is from the weak and stupid masses that the notion of objective morality originally sprang.

In *The Genealogy of Morals,* Nietzsche made his moral philosophy as clear as Nietzsche made any of his positions. Aristocrats, he claimed, once recognized in themselves the source and spring of all value. Thus, "every aristocratic morality springs from a triumphant affirmation of its own demands," "it acts and grows spontaneously," seeking "its antithesis in order to pronounce a more grateful and exultant 'yes' to its own self [.]" From within the framework of the aristocratic or "master" morality, "its negative conception, 'low,' 'vulgar,' 'bad,' is merely a pale late-born foil in comparison with its positive and fundamental conception...of 'we aristocrats, we good ones, we beautiful ones, we happy ones." Aristocrats or masters create their morality and celebrate the "life and passion" from which they do so.

The masses or "slaves" are as well creators of morality, yet their creation originates in a very different sort of impulse than that which animates aristocrats. "The revolt of the slaves in morals," Nietzsche says, "begins in the very principle of *resentment* becoming creative and giving birth to values[.]" The masses, weak, stupid, and incompetent, are motivated to exact against those who they recognize as their superiors in every respect a sort of "imaginary revenge." The slave morality, in glaring contrast to the master morality, has an "*inevitable* gravitation to the objective instead of back to the subjective [.]" It "requires as the condition of its existence an external and objective world....objective stimuli" to move it to action.[9]

Christianity, Nietzsche believes, is the penultimate expression of the slave morality.

In *Beyond Good and Evil,* Nietzsche wrote that though every person, irrespective of his morality, is "a creator" or "determiner" of values,[10] those who subscribe to the slave morality refuse to acknowledge the subjective basis of their creation. And what *is* the engine driving the creation of value? Nietzsche identifies it as "the Will to Power," or "the Will to Life."

Life is "*essentially* appropriation, injury, conquest of the strange and weak, suppression, severity, obtrusion of peculiar forms, incorporation, and at the least, putting it mildest, exploitation," and exploitation is nothing more or less than "a consequence of the intrinsic Will to Power, which is precisely the Will to Life." [11]

All living organisms seek to dominate their surroundings, and human organisms strive to create and continuously recreate the world in their image, in ways that promise to satisfy their subjective longings, their needs, desires, and interests. The proponents of the slave morality, though, refuse to acknowledge this even as they are busy advancing a worldview that, by Nietzsche's lights, is life-denying.

The 20th century French existentialist philosopher Jean-Paul Sartre is in complete agreement with not only fellow atheists like Nietzsche, but Christians, like Fyodor Dostoyevsky, who maintain that "if God didn't exist, everything would be possible." Dostoyevsky meant that unless God exists, standards of morality can only be as numerous and shifting as the grains of sand on a beach. To put it another way, God guarantees the objectivity and immutability of moral standards. For this reason, Sartre describes the human being's condition as one of "abandonment." By abandonment, Sartre explains, existentialists "merely mean to say that God does not exist, and that we must bear the full consequences of that assertion." [12] As Sartre is quick to show, the consequences of atheism are far more momentous than those like Sam Harris are willing to acknowledge.

Historically, atheists have thought it possible "to eliminate God as painlessly as possible." They have thought that "nothing will have changed if God does not exist." Harris is no exception to this rule. Sartre sums up their position. We "will encounter the same standards of honesty, progress, and humanism, and we will have turned God into an obsolete hypothesis that will die quietly on its own."

Sartre is convinced that such atheists couldn't be more mistaken. If God does not exist, he says, gone, then, is "the possibility of finding values in an intelligible." Gone as well is "any *a priori* Good [absolute, objective moral constraints, like honesty, justice, etc.], since there would be no infinite and perfect consciousness to conceive of it." Sartre drives home this point: "Nowhere is it written that good exists, that we must be honest or must not lie, since we are on a plane shared only by men."[13]

God does not exist and "man" is abandoned, "for he cannot find anything to rely on—neither within nor without. Neither within him nor without does he find anything [objective moral standards] to cling to."[14]

Tellingly, for Sartre and the atheistic existentialist philosophers whose thought he represents, the non-existence of God implies the non-existence of human nature. This is critical, for most atheists and agnostics continue to endorse some reading or other of human nature in which to anchor their reading of morality. Yet they have long since given up their justification for doing so.

Inasmuch as human nature is said to consist in a set of characteristics that are supposed to be essential to all human beings, it is conceived as a sort of model that precedes and transcends any and all *individual* humans. "When we think of God the Creator, we usually conceive of him as a superlative artisan," Sartre tells us. So, "the concept of man, in the mind of God, is comparable to the concept of a paper knife in the mind of the manufacturer: God produces man following certain techniques and a conception, just as the craftsman, following a definition and a technique, produces a paper knife." The point here is that the general or universal concept, the essence, the blueprint in the mind of the artisan precedes the creation of the individual things that are based on it.

In other words, before there are individual human beings, there is the concept, essence, or nature of humanity within the "divine intelligence."[15] But "since there is no God to conceive it," Sartre concludes, "there is no human nature [.]"[16]

While Nietzsche celebrates "the death of God," Sartre laments it. Since there is no God, "we will encounter no values or orders" that can "legitimize our conduct." Thus, "in the luminous realm of values," we find no "means of justification or excuse." The prognosis is bleak: "We are left alone and without excuse."[17]

A particularly renowned atheist and philosopher of religion was J. L. Mackie.

Mackie was convinced that there is "no doubt that some features of modern European moral concepts are traceable to the theological ethics of Christianity." He refers to "quasi-imperative notions, on what ought to be done or on what is wrong in a sense that is close to that of 'forbidden'" as "relics of divine commands."

Mackie alludes, approvingly, to the Catholic philosopher Elizabeth Anscombe who made this very point. Summarizing her position, Mackie writes that "modern…concepts of moral obligation, moral duty, of what is morally right and wrong, and of the moral sense of 'ought' are survivals outside the framework of thought that made them really intelligible, namely the belief in divine law."[18]

Since, being an atheist, Mackie disavows the existence of a Divine Lawgiver, he recognizes that it must follow that there cannot be any divine moral laws.

Mackie refers to his own position as "moral skepticism" or "subjectivism." He states it boldly: "There are no objective values."

Elaborating, Mackie leaves the reader in no doubt that in denying that objective moral values are "part of the fabric of the world," he denies not just "moral goodness...but also other things that could be more loosely called moral values or disvalues—rightness and wrongness, duty, obligation, an action's being rotten and contemptible, and so on." [19]

Mackie anticipates the most common criticism of his view, a criticism that we can as easily imagine Sam Harris leveling against it as we can imagine any average theist doing so: "How could anyone deny that there is a difference between a kind action and a cruel one, or that a coward and a brave man behave differently in the face of danger?" [20] (Or, as Harris would say, are there not self-evident differences between acts that are productive of suffering and those that conduce toward pleasure or happiness?)

Mackie's response is to the point: The critics are correct that there most so certainly are fundamental differences between these kinds of actions. But this observation is as irrelevant as it is accurate. "The kinds of behavior to which moral values and disvalues are *ascribed* are indeed part of the furniture of the world, and so are the natural, descriptive, differences between them; but not, perhaps, their differences in *value*." [21]

It's obvious that "cruel actions differ from kind ones," Mackie says, "but is it an equally hard fact that actions which are cruel in a descriptive sense are to be condemned?" There is no question regarding the objectivity of "natural, factual differences" between actions. There most certainly is, however, a question regarding the objectivity of the values that are ascribed to these actions. [22]

Mackie here distinguishes between "natural facts" and "moral facts." His goal is to show that the great 18th century Scottish philosopher David Hume was correct in claiming that, logically, the former can never entail the latter. "What is the connection between the natural fact that an action is a piece of deliberate cruelty—say, causing pain just for fun—and the moral fact that it is wrong? It cannot be an entailment, a logical or semantic necessity."

That these are, or appear to be, two fundamentally different sorts of things can be gotten easily enough when it is considered that while it is clearly with our senses that we perceive the infliction of wanton pain by one person upon another, this property of "wrongness" or "evil" or "badness" that supposedly inheres in the action does not appear to be sensuous.

At the very least, it is far from obvious that immorality is an object of sense perception. We can see Bob jab Chris in the face with a sharp instrument, and this sight followed by the sights and sounds of Chris's flesh tearing, blood oozing out, and Chris screaming in pain. But we can neither see nor hear the *immorality* of this action. If there is some necessary link between the act and its value, it is, as Mackie says, "mysterious."[23]

Mackie proposes that we needn't posit any mysterious entity or connection, for we can account for our moral judgments by looking no further than ourselves. We can make sense of "the supposed objectivity of moral values as arising from what we can call the projection or objectification of moral attitudes," of "wants and demands."[24]

In short, we have the moral attitudes that we do, attitudes that we imbibed from the societal environments within which we were reared, and so as to lend them an absolute authority that they would otherwise lack, we project them onto the world as if they inhered in the nature of things. None of this need be done consciously, and most of it is done unconsciously. But, as far as Mackie sees it, only a moral subjectivism of the sort for which he argues can surmount the paradoxes that arise from positing objective moral values.

Ultimately, ours is a morally-neutral world.

Mackie is following the path forged 200 years earlier by David Hume—who, not coincidentally, also did not believe in God. Hume insisted that, contrary to what philosophers and the laity alike have traditionally maintained, what we have here been calling moral value is a projection of the human mind upon its surroundings.

According to Hume, if moral value (virtue and vice, what's laudable and blameworthy) were beyond our own minds, then it would have to be found either in "relations of ideas" or "matters of fact." Yet he is confident that just a little reflection reveals that it is found in neither. Take the first position that moral worth resides within the relations between actions and agents. Hume supplies two illustrations to undermine it.

First, we all find parricide, the murder of a parent by his or her offspring, to be among "the most horrid and unnatural" of actions. Many are tempted to think that the evil of parricide is determined by the specific relation that obtains between the progenitor and its progeny. Why, then, do we detect no immorality in the event of a large tree being overtaken and destroyed by *its* progeny? That the parricide that occurs here is not "attended with the notion of immorality" as it is when it involves humans is proof, for Hume, that the notion of immorality "does not arise" from the discernment of the relation between parent and offspring.[25]

Or why is it that incest is considered "criminal" for subverting natural human relations but unobjectionable when it transpires between animals that are related? After all, animals "are susceptible of the same relations, with respect to each other, as the human species, and therefore would also be susceptible of the same morality, if the essence of morality consisted in these relations." That animals lack reason, Hume says, "may hinder them from perceiving the duties and obligations of morality, but" this "can never hinder these duties from existing"—if, that is, the duties are grounded in relations that animals share with humans.[26]

31

If moral value does not inhere in relations, may it not be a factual aspect of the world, i.e. a "matter of fact?" Hume shoots down this possibility in no time as well. He gives the example of "willful murder," an act that everyone recognizes as "vicious." Hume remarks: "Examine it in all lights, and see if you can find that matter of fact, or real existence, which you call *vice*. In whichever way you take it," Hume continues, "you find only certain passions, motives, volitions and thoughts. There is no other matter of fact in the case."

In other words, the viciousness of the act is not in the act per se: "The vice entirely escapes you, as long as you consider the *object*." To find the vice "you must turn your reflection into your own breast, and find a sentiment of disapprobation, which arises in you, towards this action."

This sentiment is a matter of fact, "but it is the object of feeling, not of reason. It lies in yourself, not in the object."[27] Moral value, then, is *subjective*, not *objective*.

It is at this juncture that Hume alludes to the phenomenon of what has since come to be recognized as "the naturalistic fallacy."

In "every system of morality" of which Hume is familiar, he says, there is an "imperceptible" movement on the part of the author from "the usual copulations of propositions, *is,* and *is not*" to propositions that are "entirely different from it," those "connected with an *ought,* or an *ought not.*" Logically, the move is illicit, for moral prescriptions can never be deduced from factual descriptions.

> *For as this ought, or ought not, expresses some new relation or affirmation, it is necessary that it should be observed and explained; and at the same time that a reason should be given, for what seems altogether inconceivable, how this new relation can be a deduction from others, which are entirely different from it.*[28]

Christianity and the World

We can account for our moral obligation by looking within ourselves, toward the "sentiments" of our shared human nature. Our moral obligations aren't deductions from *reason* but, rather, the function of *feeling*.

The foregoing sampling of philosophers is instructive in that it discloses how, over the span of centuries, some of the modern West's most prominent atheistic and agnostic thinkers realized that there is indeed more than an incidental or secondary connection between theism and belief in objective morality. The problem, though, with the non-objectivist ethical theories that these philosophers advanced is that, at best, they may succeed in accounting for how and why people feel that they have moral obligations.

There is, however, a world of difference between *feeling* that one has moral duties and actually *having* them. At an intuitive level, people, whether they are professional philosophers or not, "know" that moral values are real, that they are part of the furniture of the universe. No one speaks and acts in everyday life as if they thought that obligations, virtues, vices, goodness, badness, and so forth were just projections of our minds upon a cold, value-neutral world.

Immanuel Kant was one eminent philosopher that sought to align his ethical theory with this observation of how people do in fact think, speak, and act with respect to morality.

Kant revolutionized the field of philosophy. Such was the impact of his thought upon the Western tradition that it has been said that Kant achieved his own "Copernican revolution." Epistemologically, metaphysically, and ethically, Kant's contribution to the Western philosophical tradition was and remains a game-changer.

In ethics, he attempted to establish a theologically-indifferent justification for morality. To repeat, Kant sought to anchor morality in, not the will or eternal law of God, but Reason. Time and space constraints preclude a thorough analysis of Kant's ethical theory. For our purposes, it is will suffice to show that, for all of his efforts to root morals in secular foundations, and despite his insistence that neither reason nor experience could demonstrate God's existence, even Kant concluded that our obligations could be most adequately accounted for only if we "postulate" two things: the immortality of the soul and God.

For Kant, the "summum bonum," or the highest good, is what he calls "the moral law," a law of reason. It is from the moral law that we deduce our duties, obligations to self and others that are absolute, unconditional. Kant tells us that the "achievement of the highest good in the world is the necessary object of a will determinable by the moral law." However, "the complete fitness of intentions to the moral law is the supreme condition of the highest good."

To put it another way, the highest good, the moral law, will be implemented if and only if people never fail to respect the moral law and to enact its requirements from this respect. The problem, though, is that "complete fitness of the will to the moral law is holiness," and the latter is "a perfection of which no rational being in the world of sense is at any time capable."

For as dutiful as even the most dutiful of people may be, no one, in this world of ours, is perfect. Nevertheless, to say of a person that he *ought* to do such-and-such implies that he *can* do it.

We needn't look far before we encounter any number of examples from everyday life that reinforce this principle that "ought implies can."

All things considered, it is at once reasonable and just for me to penalize a student for not doing his homework. The penalty presupposes both that the student had an obligation to do his homework—he ought to have done it—as well that he could have executed this obligation. On the other hand, if I assigned the homework retrospectively, when no student could have known about it, then it would be most unreasonable and unjust for me to penalize any of my students for not submitting it. In the latter case, there was no obligation to do the homework because students could not have done it. Kant's point is that a duty implies the ability of the duty-bound person to fulfill it.

Yet if it is impossible for us to live in perfect accordance with the moral law *in this life,* if we cannot be motivated to fulfill all of our duties from a respect for the moral law while we inhabit this world; and if we do in fact have an obligation to do just this, then "it is required as practically necessary" that we suppose that we will have eternity to do what we must. "But since it [the realization of the moral law] is required as practically necessary, it can be found only in an endless progress to that complete fitness [.]"[29] And this "infinite progress is possible…only under the presupposition of an infinitely enduring existence and personality of the same rational being [.]" The latter, Kant tells us, "is called the immortality of the soul."

So, only if we live forever can we accomplish what we are morally required to accomplish. "Thus, the highest good is practically possible only on the supposition of the immortality of the soul [.]"[30]

If we are immortal souls, then we *can* do what we *ought* to do because we will have eternity to do it.

We must also suppose the existence of God, for within the notion of the moral law is the idea that those who endeavor to act rightly should have happiness. That is, implied in the concept of the moral law is the idea that those who conform their minds and wills to it are *deserving* or *worthy* of happiness.

Kant insists that "there is not the slightest ground in the moral law for a necessary connection between the morality and proportionate happiness of a being which belongs to the world,"[31] that "morals is not really the doctrine how we should *make* ourselves happy but of how we should be *worthy* of happiness."[32]

Still, it is intrinsic to the concept of a moral order that happiness and moral goodness coincide. This in turn demands that we postulate "a cause of the whole of nature, itself distinct from nature, which contains the ground of the exact coincidence of happiness with morality."

The conviction that morality and perfect happiness must ultimately coincide demands the existence of a being, an omniscient and omnibenevolent being, that can make it happen. It demands the existence of God.[33]

George Mavrodes is a contemporary philosopher who elaborated on Kant's insight that inasmuch as we really have moral duties, i.e. actions that we must perform irrespectively of our inclinations to the contrary and regardless of whether we reap any discernible benefits from doing so, then a materialist conception of reality like that which Harris defends becomes problematic.

Mavrodes cites a passage from the famed atheist philosopher Bertrand Russell. Russell supplies the proverbial (and literal) textbook illustration of the materialist view of the cosmos. In terms of its key respects that he identifies, neither Harris nor any other materialist would or could find a thing with which to quibble. They are: (1) Humans are "the product of causes which had no prevision of the end they were achieving," all "hopes and fears," "loves" and "beliefs" being "but the outcome of accidental collocations of atoms"; (2) There is no life "beyond the grave"; and (3) Once this world becomes extinct, which it will, "the whole temple of man's achievement must inevitably be buried beneath the debris of a universe in ruins [.]"[34]

But as Mavrodes observes, if the world is ultimately, most fundamentally, just matter in motion, then this fails to account for our shared sense that we really have obligations. Materialism fails utterly to answer the question that in some form or other ethicists have been wrestling over from at least the time that Socrates first posed it: Why strive to be moral?

Note, the issue here is not a puzzle as to why people should *act* morally. As Socrates' interlocutor Glaucon pointed out, it doesn't require much wisdom to recognize that only if one *appears* to be good and just will one avoid undesirable social and legal

Christianity and the World

repercussions. The challenge here is determining reasons to justify the quest to *be* good and just. The challenge for the materialist, with his atheistic worldview, is more daunting than it is for most.

Recall, an obligation or duty is something that exists regardless of whether it is accompanied by an inclination to perform it. Nor does an obligation depend upon the material and/or social consequences that are expected to ensue upon performance or non-performance of the act.

This last point is particularly telling, for as Mavrodes correctly notes, there is no small number of times when fulfilling an obligation will not only fail to bestow upon the actor the only sorts of benefits that a materialist, atheist universe has to offer, but cause the agent to suffer. "Pleasure, happiness, esteem, contentment, self-realization, knowledge—all of these can suffer from the fulfillment of a moral obligation."[35]

Real morality, then, as opposed to cultural convention and subjective preference, is objective. Harris seems to recognize this. Yet, his presumption to the contrary aside, Harris's atheistic theory fails entirely to provide an objective grounding for morality as he conceives it.

Actually, it is questionable whether he describes a morality at all.

It's crucial to realize that in saying of morality that it is objective is not equivalent to describing it as *intersubjective* or *interpersonal*. The objective, in other words, is not tantamount to consensus.

Nor is the morally objective to be equated with what "works" or what brings people pleasure.

A truly objective morality must consist of norms or imperatives that are independent of peoples' wishes, likes, and dislikes. These imperatives are independent of their wills. The human inclination to avert pain and pursue pleasure or "happiness" (whatever exactly this means) may lend some insight as to human *wants, instincts, appetites,* and *desires.* However, this tells us nothing regarding human *obligations, rights,* and *virtues.*

Knowing what people *want* is not the same as knowing what they *ought* to do. From the knowledge that people *value, desire,* or even *need* X we go no distance toward knowing whether they are morally entitled to X. Harris seems to elide this most fundamental of distinctions between the merely descriptive and the normative.

Indeed, it is doubtful that Harris can be said to be referring to *morality* given his likening of humans to animals. Animals are most definitely *not* "generally intolerant of murder and theft," "deception" and "sexual betrayal." This is because *there is no murder, deception, and betrayal among animals.*

If animals were moral agents, this would mean that they would have moral obligations, which they clearly do not. Moral agency presupposes self-consciousness, rationality, and language. Only by way of such faculties can moral agency come about because it is through precisely these faculties that moral actors acquire *knowledge* of the concepts of right, wrong, good, bad, evil, responsibility, duty, obligation, justice, and so forth. Only beings with these capacities can *reflect* upon possible courses of action and evaluate them not just for their prospective efficiency vis-à-vis the attainment of the agent's goals, but for their moral import.

Lions do not *murder* wildebeest and gazelles. They kill their prey, certainly, but only a moral simpleton would think to equate all instances of killing with instances of murder. Murder is, by definition, unjustified or indefensible killing, and since only beings that are, in theory, capable of arguing in their own defense can be said to have acted defensibly or not, animals, who lack the reason and language to advocate on their own behalf, cannot act wrongly. There is no murder, lying, or any other moral failing amongst animals.

When Harris says of animals that they are "intolerant" of moral evils he convicts himself of the grossest anthropomorphism, for he projects onto animals characteristics that they do not and cannot possess. Animals have *instincts* for self-preservation and the propagation of their species, yet instincts are not knowledge. At any rate, instincts do not comprise *moral* knowledge or sensibility.

Harris asserts that human beings want to avert suffering and achieve happiness. It is obvious, he says, that love facilitates happiness while hate detracts from it. Thus, even from within the parameters of his atheistic vision of the cosmos, Harris assures us, there are objective reasons for preferring love to hatred.

There are several problems with this position.

The first is that while people undoubtedly do desire "happiness," this is hardly the only thing that they desire. People as well desire knowledge, virtue, and any number of other activities. Pleasure may accompany their pursuit of such goods. This, though, does not mean that it was for the sake of pleasure that they initially engaged in these pursuits. In fact, as critics of hedonism have long noted, a person can't know whether such-and-such an activity brings him or her satisfaction until *after* he or she has engaged in it.

In short, a person must be motivated by considerations other than those of personal edification to engage in an activity for the first time.

There is, however, another point. Just because a person values X does not mean that he *should* value X, it does not mean that X itself is valuable. Harris, recall, suggests that a belief in God (or, as he incorrectly puts it, "the Bible") is unnecessary for morality. That people pursue pleasure and avoid pain is the only ground or foundation for an objective morality that we need. This, though, will not do.

There are two senses, a subjective and objective, in which we can speak of something as being valuable. According to the subjective sense, something is valuable simply and solely because there are people who value it. In contrast, to say in the objective sense that something is valuable is to say that regardless of whether anyone actually does in fact value it, the thing in question is nonetheless intrinsically valuable.

Yet something that a person values, that, subjectively, he or she finds good, may be objectively bad. It may be the case that the person shouldn't desire or pursue it.

Thirdly, even assuming that people should pursue "happiness," this by itself goes no distance toward specifying *which activities* they should seek so as to obtain happiness. And even if it did provide insight into the latter, *that* in turn would offer no guidance as to *how* one should go about procuring them. The knowledge that we should seek pleasure or even specific pleasures entails no criteria for distinguishing between permissible and impermissible ways of achieving our ends.

Fourthly, Harris, however, *does* try to abstract criteria from his reading of human nature. Since, he says, love is conducive to a person's happiness while hatred detracts from it, persons should conduct themselves lovingly. This love, in turn, will not infrequently demand of people that they act self-sacrificially for those whom they love. With this move, problems abound.

One difficulty is that when love and hatred are treated, as Harris treats them, as *feelings* or *motives* to action, it is impossible to determine in advance the specific actions that an agent will or should take. Feelings like love, hatred, resentment, greed, envy, affection, admiration, and so forth are concepts that, as such, are intractably vague, concepts that, to paraphrase the philosopher Ronald Dworkin, admit of many *conceptions*. But there are other challenges.

Any action is, in principle, compatible with any of these feelings: People—not Harris, but at least some of those whom he derides—pray for those for whom they feel revulsion, those whom they consider their enemies. Contrary to the profoundly oversimplified, sentimentalist idea of love to which Harris alludes, in the real world it is a tragic fact that self-sacrifice is not the only type of conduct that love motivates. For the sake of those whom they love, people can and have lied, cheated, and stolen. Love can and has driven people to harm and even murder those perceived as threats to the objects of their love. In fact, in the name of love, people have beaten and murdered those *who they love*.

"Love" and "hatred," taken in themselves, supply no guidance to moral conduct.

Another, more fundamental problem, we have already seen: description, without further ado, cannot justify prescription. Even if it is true that people will be motivated to act lovingly and avoid acting hatefully in their journey to obtain happiness and avert pain, respectively, their inclinations are distinct from their duties.

That I love so-and-so or such-and-such does not mean that I *ought* to have this love. The love that motivates a battered woman to remain within an abusive relationship is not commendable. She loves her abuser. This, though, doesn't mean that she *should* love him. Harris commits what philosophers have long recognized as the "naturalistic fallacy," the logical pitfall into which a person plummets when presuming to deduce ethical prescriptions from (allegedly) factual descriptions.

If morality is real, then it demands objectivity. Even Sam Harris acknowledges this. However, this being so, atheistic, agnostic, and theistic thinkers from throughout the centuries until the present have conceded that a supreme moral legislator, the ultimate source and standard of the Right and the Good, i.e. God, is the most plausible ground in which to anchor morality. Once God's existence is rejected, belief in an objective moral order becomes impossible to sustain. Harris's own theory, for the reasons noted, is wholly inadequate to establishing the objectivity of morality.

My purpose above was to show that Harris's moral critique of Christianity backfires, that the universal experience of morality forces us to look beyond it to an objective ground of which God is the most eligible candidate. I further sought to show that the purportedly ethical theory that Harris seeks to substitute for the traditional theistic one fails on its own terms.

There are, of course, other arguments that Harris launches in his offensive against Christian theism. Considering, however, that the "new atheists" speak in one voice, for some of these other criticisms we can turn to Richard Dawkins.

CHAPTER III

The Rational Defensibility of Christianity and the Atheism's Weak Case Against It

RICHARD DAWKINS, LIKE Harris, is a scientist by trade. Specifically, Dawkins is a biologist. He should have remained within his field rather than address theological and philosophical questions for which he is ill-equipped to deal. This is not meant to be an insult. The painful truth of the matter is that Dawkins, like Harris, displays, quite literally, incredible ineptitude when engaging an issue, like the existence of God, that requires a level of philosophical sophistication exceeding that of a college freshman. Here, we shall limit our focus on Dawkins' sophomoric mischaracterizations of some of the traditional "proofs" for God's existence and his replies to the strawmen that he constructs.

Throughout the centuries, Christian philosophers have formulated multiple rational arguments, "proofs," for God. Some of these arguments, like "the argument from motion," have their origins in the pre-Christian, pagan world of ancient Greek philosophy. While individually they have drawn the line in different ways, Christians as a whole have always recognized a distinction between the realms of "reason" and "faith." Those who contributed to the development of proofs supposed that while some ideas, like those of the Incarnation, the Holy Trinity, and so forth, can be known only through faith, others, like the existence of God, could be determined by reason alone. Arguments of the latter sort belong to what is called "natural theology."

One such argument is the "ontological" proof. First formulated by (Saint) Anselm of Canterbury in the 11th century, the ontological argument isn't just the most controversial of arguments *for God's existence*; it is undoubtedly one of the most controversial arguments *in all of Western philosophy*. To this day, much ink continues to be spilt over it—a fact that alone attests to its thoughtfulness. Even its opponents respect it enough to engage it and, importantly, it has its defenders.

The ontological argument is an *a priori* argument, a proof based on pure thought. Its conclusion affirming God's existence is deduced from reflection on the very idea or definition of the Supreme Being; the argument makes no appeals to experience.

Anselm's reasoning is as follows: Both the theist and the atheist, the believer and the unbeliever, share the same concept of God as "a being than which none greater can be conceived." Both recognize that in affirming and denying God's existence, respectively, they affirm and deny, respectively, the existence of the greatest or best conceivable being. The atheist no less than the theist knows that God is, by definition, the greatest or supreme being.

Of course, they fundamentally disagree insofar as the atheist thinks that this greatest being is just an idea in the mind, the product of the imagination, while the theist believes that God is both an idea in the mind and an actual being. Who is correct?

Anselm's response is to the point: The theist must be correct, for a being that exists in both the mind and in reality is greater than a being that exists only in the mind. Thus, God, the greatest of beings, *must* exist.

God *necessarily* exists.[1]

Dawkins refers to the ontological argument—an argument, mind you, that he himself acknowledges has been treated with seriousness by some of the most astute of philosophical minds, including those of atheists—as "infantile"[2] and "logomachist trickery [.]" It is mere "wordplay" exploited to justify "a grand truth about the cosmos [.]" Immanuel Kant and David Hume, two world-renown 18th century philosophers, offered "the most definitive refutations" of Anselm's position, Dawkins informs his readers.[3]

Actually, while Hume and Kant (but particularly the latter) offered objections that were both thought-provoking and famous, they were hardly the decisive answers to the ontological argument that Dawkins would have us think they are.

For Hume, all knowledge is reducible to two types. The first consists in what Hume described as "relations of ideas." The second pertains to "matters of fact." Relations of ideas involve purely logical or a prior relations between concepts. "Bachelors are unmarried males," "Green Martians are colored beings," and "If X is bigger than Y and Y is bigger than Z, then X is bigger than Z" are all examples of relations of ideas. The latter are universally and necessarily true, meaning that the denial of a proposition expressing a relation of ideas entails a contradiction. "Green Martians are color*less* beings" does not just happen to be false; it is necessarily false. Not in any possible world could anything that is green (or any other color) be colorless at the same moment. Propositions encapsulating relations of ideas need not have any correlation with any aspects of the world as it happens to actually exist.

In contrast, statements asserting "matters of fact" may or may not be true—they are never necessarily true. The truth of a matter of fact is contingent upon the way the world actually is at the moment that the statement is made. The truth of the statement, "Carla was present in class today," is contingent upon whether Carla was in fact present in class. If she was absent, then while the statement would be false, it would just happen to be false. In other circumstances, namely, on a day when Carla was actually present, the statement would be true.

There is no contradiction involved in denying a statement expressing a matter of fact. And, unlike statements expressing relations of ideas, matters of fact are not a priori. To know whether a statement embodying a matter of fact is true, experience is required. Hence, matters of fact are a posteriori.

Hume insists that existential propositions—statements affirming and denying *the existence* of things—are *always* matters of fact. They are, then, never necessarily true. They are not a priori. Knowledge of existence is grounded in experience.

So, Anselm's assumption to the contrary notwithstanding, "God exists" is not a relation of ideas. Its denial, "God does not exist," is not the self-contradiction that Anselm construes it as. *If* God exists, then this can be known only through experience—which the ontological argument excludes.[4]

Hume was hardly the first philosopher to object to the ontological argument. And he was far from the first to maintain that God's existence could be known only through experience. Christian thinkers, *medieval* Christian thinkers, preceded him by centuries on both of these counts.

In the 13th century, Thomas Aquinas, one of the two most renowned Christian philosophers and among the most prominent philosophers that the world had ever produced, rejected the ontological argument on the grounds that no actual existents could ever be deduced from pure thought. Anselm incorrectly, Aquinas believed, treated the proposition affirming God's existence as if it was as axiomatic as a proposition affirming that a triangle has three sides. It is not. This is why people have been able to deny God's existence, while they could never coherently deny that a triangle has three sides. If God's existence is to be established, he continued, it would have to be by way of an argument to the best explanation from our shared experience of the world.

Nevertheless, Aquinas claimed that while "God exists" is not self-evident *to us,* it is indeed self-evident *in itself.* Aquinas drew an analogy to illustrate this distinction between two senses in which something could be said to be self-evident. The statement "Incorporeal things do not exist in a place" is self-evident in itself but not to us. Most people do not know what "incorporeal" means, and even after they are informed that an incorporeal being is a non-physical being, it will doubtless require an exercise in reflection of a type to which they are unaccustomed to realize that, necessarily, a non-physical being cannot occupy space.

The statement is self-evident; it is necessarily true. But it is self-evident in itself—not to most of us. "God exists," Thomas thought, is logically comparable in this regard.[5]

The difference, then, between Aquinas and Hume is that while both rejected the ontological argument, agreeing that experience is, in some way, indispensable to one's knowledge of God, Aquinas recognized that a perfect being is a unique being insofar as it is the only being that, depending upon nothing else, exists *essentially.* As the medieval theorists put it, in God essence and existence are one. So, "God exists" isn't just true; it is necessarily true.

Hume is correct that when it comes to anything that happens to exist, i.e. a human being, a chair, a house, etc., anything the knowledge of which must include a knowledge of that which is responsible for having brought it into being, than experience is mandatory. But the perfect being, a self-sufficient being, in essence or by definition depends upon nothing for its existence or conservation. Knowledge of such a being's existence, thus, can be a priori.

Or, to put it in Hume's terminology, there is a "relation" between the idea of the greatest conceivable being, on the one hand, and that of its necessary existence, on the other.

In the 1700s, Gottfried Leibniz reformulated the ontological argument. No doubt, Dawkins would be inclined to dismiss him as an idiot and conman for subscribing to and peddling such "infantile" and "logomachist trickery," but in reality Leibniz was a logician, student of physics, and mathematician who was the first to invent the calculus. Such was the impressiveness of Leibniz's contributions to a bewildering range of intellectual pursuits that even his opponents were compelled to admire his genius. Denis Diderot, for instance, an atheist, metaphysical materialist, wrote of Leibniz in the *Encyclopedia*: "Perhaps never has a man read as much, studied as much, meditated more, and written more than Leibniz." His compositions on "the world, God, nature, and the soul" are "of the most sublime eloquence."

Diderot went so far as to remark that when "one compares the talents one has with those of a Leibniz, one is tempted to throw away one's books and go die quietly in the dark of some forgotten corner." [6]

Leibniz contended that before the ontological argument could hope to succeed, its proponents first had to show that the idea of God, the greatest conceivable being, was possible. They had to show that the idea of God was not self-contradictory. There is nothing self-contradictory or incoherent, Leibniz reasoned, within the idea of a perfect being, a being that necessarily exists.

Thus, such an idea is conceivable or possible. But if the idea of a necessary being is possible, then a necessary being in fact exists, for a necessary being that is only possible *is* a contradiction in terms. "There may or may not exist a being that must exist" is incoherent.

Thus, God necessarily exists. [7]

Kant objected to the ontological argument on the grounds that, allegedly, it presupposes a fundamental misunderstanding of the concept of existence. Existence, Kant declared, is not a "predicate." A predicate is the grammatical analogue of a property or characteristic. Predicates serve a specific function: they describe subjects. For example, in the sentence, "Bob is tall," the predicate-term, "tall," distinguishes the subject-term, "Bob," from those subjects that are not tall. The predicate-term, in other words, augments our understanding of the subject-term. To know that Bob *exists,* however, is to know virtually nothing, for the thought of Bob as existing and that of Bob as not existing are, conceptually, one and the same idea. Existence fails to differentiate one thing from another.

Kant gave the following example to make this point. Imagine, he said, one hundred real dollars. Then imagine one hundred imaginary dollars. In thought, the two are indistinguishable. Matters are quite otherwise, however, if we were to imagine, say, one hundred *red* dollars followed by one hundred *green* dollars, or one hundred *wrinkled* dollars succeeded by one hundred *non*-wrinkled dollars, for in these instances, we have the benefit of predicates—red, green, wrinkled, non-wrinkled—to distinguish the subjects in question.[8]

While Kant's criticism is certainly famous, it is most definitely not the decisive refutation of the ontological argument that Dawkins would have us believe it is. In fact, it is about as controversial as the ontological argument itself.

Some, like the mathematical-logician and philosopher, Gottlieb Frege,[9] and the atheist philosopher Bertrand Russell,[10] maintained that existence *is* a predicate, but a "second-order" predicate, a property predicated of, not *individuals,* but *concepts* and *propositional functions*, respectively. For instance, in the sentence, "There are no unicorns," non-existence is not a property that is assigned to unicorns. Rather, the concept of a unicorn is the subject, and what is being said here is that the concept of a unicorn is not instantiated in the real world. So, "The concept of the unicorn has no real-world instances," is a meaningful proposition with a subject, the concept of a unicorn, and a predicate, "has no real-world instances."

Others have responded to Kant by stating that *even if* he is correct and existence is not a predicate of any kind, his observation is utterly irrelevant to the ontological argument. It is on this reply that we should focus.

Interestingly, Dawkins quotes philosopher of religion Norman Malcolm as if to suggest that the latter found the ontological argument just as ludicrous as Dawkins declares it to be. "The doctrine that existence is a perfection is remarkably queer," Malcolm said. "It makes sense and is true to say that my future house will be a better one if it is insulated than if it is not insulated; but what could it mean to say that it will be a better house if it exists than if it does not?"[11]

But far from being a critic, Malcolm defended the ontological argument. He noted that in his original formulation, Anselm contended not that existence was always better than non-existence but, rather, that *necessary* existence is superior to *contingent* existence: a being that must exist, that cannot not exist, is superior to a being that, depending upon others, may not exist.[12]

Malcolm is scarcely the only contemporary philosopher to defend some version or other of the ontological argument. The point here, though, is not that the ontological argument ultimately succeeds. The verdict is still out on this. The point, rather, is to show that minds far more philosophically and theologically adept than anything that Dawkins has displayed recognize in the ontological argument a species of reasoning that deserves to be treated with the utmost seriousness. Dawkins' judgment that it is "infantile," "logomachist," and mere "wordplay" is the function of the pseudo-intellectualism and sophomoric attitude with which he addresses topics that transcend his area of expertise.

Thomas Aquinas, one of the two most preeminent philosophers from the middle ages, thought that those who wished to show that God's existence is rationally defensible must appeal first and foremost to undeniable aspects of our shared human

Christianity and the World

experience. He appeals specifically to five phenomena to show that God exists. Hence, Thomas's is known as the "five ways" argument.[13]

The first way is that of motion, by which Thomas means change. Change is a self-evident feature of our world. Whenever anything changes, it "moves" from a state of "potentiality" to a state of "actuality." But whatever is in a state of potentiality is in a state of passivity: it cannot do anything, it cannot act. So, for an actually hot piece of steel, say, to move or change from being potentially cold to actually cold, it must be changed or moved by something that already is actually cold, something like, say, ice. Nothing can change or move itself, because whatever changes is initially in a state of potentiality, and whatever is in a state of potentiality is passive.

Thomas's conclusion is that in order to account for the fact there are any things that change or move now, there must have been a first mover. An infinite regression in the series of movers is impossible. But this first mover, because it is the first, cannot itself have been moved by anything else. This first mover, then, cannot be a mixture of potentiality and actuality, but pure act, an "unmoved mover."

And this first mover, Thomas declares, is God.

His second and third ways are logically identical to the first, even though their respective points of focus are distinct.

The second way is the way of "efficient" causality. An *efficient* cause, for Thomas, is what most of us today think of when we think of a cause per se. Ours is a world comprised of efficient causes and their effects, and the former are always distinct from the latter. Thus, nothing can be the efficient cause of itself, for then it would have to exist prior to itself which, as Thomas notes, is absurd. Hence, so as to avoid an infinite regression in the series of causes and explain how there are any effects at the present moment, we must posit the existence of a first efficient cause. Being the first cause, it must in turn be *uncaused*.

The first cause or "Uncaused Cause" is God.

The third way is the way of "contingency" and "necessity." A contingent being is a being—like a human, a tree, a building, or a dog—that depends upon other things for its existence. Contingent beings, Thomas says, begin to exist at some point in time (humans, for example, begin to exist only after their parents have begotten them). If, however, the *only* beings that ever existed were contingent, as atheists maintain, then at some point there would have been *no* beings. Yet if there were no beings *then,* there would be no beings *now,* for from nothing, comes nothing.

Hence, to account for the existence of any contingent beings right now, we must have recourse to a being that is *not* contingent, a being whose existence is *necessary.*

An infinite regression of contingent beings is just as logically impossible as an infinite regression of movers and efficient causes. There must be a first being and that being, given that it is the first, cannot be contingent upon any others. The first being has to be a necessarily existent being.

This, Thomas concludes, is God.

Dawkins is not impressed. These arguments, supposing as they do the logical impossibility of an infinite regress, "make the entirely unwarranted assumption that God himself is immune to the regress." Dawkins adds that even allowing "the dubious luxury of arbitrarily conjuring up a terminator to an infinite regress and giving it a name, simply because we need one, there is absolutely no reason to endow the terminator with any of the properties," like omnipotence, omniscience, omnipresence, omnibenevolence, and so forth, that are "normally ascribed to God."

Much less are we justified in inferring from the argument the existence of a being who listens to prayers, forgives sins, and reads our "innermost thoughts."[14] A few comments are in order here.

First, neither Thomas Aquinas nor anyone else who ever made this kind of argument for God's existence—this would include Aristotle and such Islamic philosophers as Avicenna[15]—

ever denied the possibility of *some* infinite regressions. The series of numbers, after all, has no terminus.

The proponents of this argument also conceded the logical *possibility* that the universe is without beginning (For Aristotle, this wasn't just a possibility; it was an actuality). Had Dawkins been inclined to do so, he could have availed himself of the substantial body of literature on this topic to realize that it is far more nuanced than the caricature that he presents. For our purposes, suffice it to say that, broadly speaking, there are two ways in which to think about the argument against the possibility of infinite regression.

If we have in mind a series considered in terms of its *individual* members, with each preceding and succeeding the others, then it is indeed possible that such a series could extend back infinitely. In other words, to characterize it in imagistic terms, a *horizontal* infinite regression is possible.

However, if we are conceiving of the series *compositely,* as a whole, then an infinite regression of causes and/or contingent beings, a *vertical* infinite regression, is not possible. An actual infinitude of beings—an infinite number of beings co-existing simultaneously—is inconceivable, while a potential infinitude, a successive series, is not.

Even the 14th century thinker William of Ockham, who insisted against Thomas and others that God's existence was not rationally demonstrable, contended that if we think of a series, not in terms of *causes,* but of *conservers,* with each member conserving and being conserved by others, then an actual infinitude was impossible and the existence of a first or ultimate conserver certain (though Ockham didn't think that it could be demonstrated that this first conserver was God).[16]

In short, contra Dawkins, there is nothing at all "arbitrary" in insisting upon the need for a terminus so as to prevent those infinite regressions that seem logically impossible.

Second, Dawkins accuses Thomas and other proponents of the argument against infinite regression of making the "entirely unwarranted assumption that God himself is immune to the regress." This, though, is not an unwarranted assumption at all. As everyone, including Dawkins, knows, "God" is the name that we use to refer to *the* Supreme Being. From the concept of a supreme being, some implications most definitely appear to follow.

One such implication that is especially relevant here is that of *independence*: The perfect being, necessarily, depends upon no other beings for its existence. This means that God could not have been born or otherwise generated. God is not and could not be conserved by other beings from moment to moment. And God is, literally, inextinguishable.

The idea, then, that God would also have to be susceptible to the regress is absurd for three reasons: (1) only an absolutely independent being, God, is an eligible candidate to prevent an infinite regression; (2) the proposition that an absolutely independent being depends upon other causes is a contradiction in terms; and (3) to say that even God, an absolutely independent being, is not immune to the regress is to say that an infinite regression—meaning, recall, an *actual* infinitude of simultaneously existent contingent beings or conservers, *is* possible.

Third, Dawkins scoffs at the notion that "omnipotence" (all-powerful) and "omniscience" (all-knowing) can be deduced from the knowledge that there is a being—first mover, first cause, intrinsically necessary or absolutely independent—upon whom the entire universe depends for its existence. However, there's clearly nothing in the least unreasonable about it. A being that could create the cosmos from nothing would be nothing if not of unlimited power and knowledge. The case has even been made that a being that created the conditions necessary to make our universe hospitable to life must also be of unimaginable benevolence.

Christianity and the World

There is an objection to this line to which Dawkins could have recourse: There could be an infinity of universes, a "multiverse," and our universe, some have said, could be contingent upon another universe, which in turn could be contingent upon another, and so forth and so on ad infinitum.

Theoretically, this is most certainly a conceivable state of affairs. Just as there is no logical impediment to conceiving of an infinite regression of the individual members of our universe, so neither is there any such impediment to thinking of an infinite regression of universes—as long as these universes succeed each other in time. If, though, an infinite amount of coexistent universes is the referent here, then this is just as impossible as an infinite amount of actually co-existent individuals. To put it another way, this objection just pushes back the original problem one step.

Or the difficulty with this response can be put another way. A universe is not something over and above the sum totality of its parts. "Universe" is just a short-hand term for *everything,* or *all things.* This being so, whether we are dealing with one contingent being or an infinitude of contingent beings, and whether these beings are individuals or whole worlds, whatever is contingent inescapably points beyond itself to something upon which, ultimately, it depends.

As Roman Catholic priest and historian of philosopher Frederick Coppleston memorably made the point, whether there is a single piece of chocolate or countless numbers of chocolate, from chocolate only chocolate comes.[17] Similarly, whatever is contingent must, in the final analysis, yield something that is not contingent, something whose existence is necessary and upon which all other beings depend.

There is another reply to this argument for God's existence that David Hume made in the 18th century. Hume said that, since it's correct that the universe is nothing more than the sum total of its parts, we arrive at "the cause" of the universe inasmuch as we determine the cause or causes of each of its members. Hume drew an analogy between the universe and a set or marbles.

To know about a particular set of marbles, all that is required is that the inquirer determine the relations between the individual marbles that constitute the set. If, upon completing this task, someone was to say that while we now know all that there is to know about each and every individual member of the set, we are still ignorant of the cause of the set or series itself, a remotely reasonable person would conclude that the person has fundamentally misunderstood the matter at hand.

There is nothing to which the term "set" really refers other than the totality of the marbles. The only sense in which there can be said to be a "set" is mental: Through an act of the imagination, a kind of act that always involves some measure of arbitrariness, we unite objects in terms of their proximity, similarities, and so forth. There is no difference in the case of the world: The universe is just a psychologically constructed set of all things that exist.[18]

Hume's criticism does not speak to the argument from the impossibility of a *vertical* infinite regression of contingent beings, a literal infinitude of simultaneous existents. Beyond this, even if his analogy succeeded in showing that each part of the universe could be explained by reference to other parts, it would still fail to address the more fundamental question: Why are there are *any* parts at all? Why is there *something* rather than *nothing*? This is not a question that can be asked by pointing out that X depends upon or is caused by Y, which depends upon or is caused by Z, and so on.

Fourthly, Dawkins says that Aquinas's argument(s) for God goes no distance toward establishing the existence of a being that listens to prayers, forgives sins, and reads "innermost thoughts." On this score, he is absolutely correct—and Aquinas would have been the first to agree with him.

Aquinas recognized that the realms of reason and faith, though mutually complimentary, were nevertheless distinct. Both are sources of truth, but there are truths that only faith can reveal. Thomas believed that while reason was sufficient to demonstrate God's existence, only faith could disclose other aspects of God's nature. That God became incarnate in Jesus; that He is Three Persons in One (the Holy Trinity); and that He expects prayers and forgives sins are truths of faith.

Dawkins and those atheists whose impulses he represents will doubtless mock this appeal to faith. They shouldn't, for contrary to a misconception that, regrettably, is as pervasive among theists as it is among atheists, faith is no more foreign to the latter than it is to the former.

To put it bluntly, atheists, particularly atheists like Dawkins and Sam Harris, live by faith too.

They have faith in the old Jewish-Christian metaphysic, faith in the notion that the universe is rational and orderly, governed by laws that make knowledge of it possible. This in turn implies that they have faith that both knowledge and truth generally are attainable.

They have faith that between their thoughts about reality and reality itself there is correspondence.

They have faith that *they* have truth and knowledge.

They have faith that progress in human affairs, in learning and in morality, are possible.

They have faith that there once lived a man named Charles Darwin and that this man became famous for fathering an "evolutionary" theory of the origins of life.

That atheists like Harris and Dawkins write books and articles; that they teach and marry and foster human relationships—all of this proves that they have faith in life's possibilities.

As the author of one quite popular book put it, "The faith of the heart, our primordial faith, is something we have all experienced in our peak moments of aliveness." This faithfulness is experienced through "simple trust, as confidence; trust in life; confidence that we won't be let down."[19] Faith doesn't require a blind leap, and its object is not limited to that which is recognizably "religious." To live is to have faith that living is at once possible and desirable.

The last two of Thomas's five ways are the ways from excellence or perfection and harmony or order, respectively. The former goes as thus: In our world, we recognize that some things are more and less beautiful, good, true, just—comprehensively, valuable. But *more* and *less* presuppose a *maximum,* a standard by which degrees of perfection or value are measured. Thomas also thought that there could only be gradations of value if there is an absolute source from which things derive what value they possess.

The way from perfection, like each of the other four ways, centers in the theme of contingency. Thomas assumes that if there are finite instances of value, things that happen to be of value, then they must be dependent upon infinite, self-sufficient perfection—which Aquinas equates with God.

The argument can best be understood by way of an analogy. Suppose that we have two stones. One of these stones has been lying in the sun for hours. The other has been in a dark cave. Clearly, the first stone will be warmer than the other. In fact, it will be very hot. However, for as warm as this stone is, it could always be warmer. Conversely, for as cool as is the stone from the cave, it retains some heat. The sun, which is maximally hot, serves as both the standard by which we can compare and contrast the degrees of heat in the stones as well as the source of their heat.

These "imperfect" or finite instances of heat point beyond themselves to something that is far greater in heat.

Dawkins views this argument contemptuously. "That's an argument?" he facetiously asks. "You might as well say, people vary in smelliness but we can make the comparison only by reference to a perfect maximum of conceivable smelliness.

Therefore there must exist a pre-eminently peerless stinker, and we call him God. Or substitute any dimension of comparison you like, and derive an equivalently fatuous conclusion."[20]

Whether Thomas's argument from perfection ultimately succeeds remains as debatable as whether his other arguments for God's existence are successful. My objective in responding to Dawkins' criticisms of these "proofs" is not to show that the latter accomplish their purpose. Rather, my objective is to reveal the intellectual flaccidity, indeed, the intellectual dishonesty, of Dawkins' criticisms. I want for the reader to realize that Dawkins, like Harris and the "new atheists" generally, are in effect no different from shadow boxers in swinging at targets that exist only to the degree that shadows and strawmen can be said to exist. His dismissal of the argument from perfection is a classic case in point.

Whether a fragrance is "smelly" or not is determined by the individual subject who experiences it as such. "Smelliness," in other words, is a subjective experience. Moreover, smelliness is not a "perfection," a property that is better to possess than to lack.

Though you wouldn't know it from reading Dawkins' account, Thomas explicitly states that his argument is meant to show that "there must also be something, which is to all beings the cause of their being, goodness, and every other *perfection* [.]" The argument from perfection begins with what he takes to be the self-evident observation that there exists in our world *beings,* some of which are more or less virtuous than one another, but none of which is perfectly virtuous.

It also relies on the assumption, no less self-evident to the inhabitants of the ancient and medieval worlds (whether the latter were Jewish, Christian, or Islamic), that being is not only itself a good, but, as Peter Kreeft puts it, "the source and condition of all value" and, thus, the most fundamental of goods or perfections.

And while this insight may not be self-evident to many moderns, we do indeed recognize it for the truth that it is insofar as we realize that, for example, long, stable, healthy lives are superior to those that are chaotic, unhealthy, and which end prematurely.

We realize that being or existence is superior to nonbeing.[21] Kreeft elaborates:

> And so we recognize the inherent superiority of all those ways of being that expand possibilities, free us from the constricting confines of matter, and allow us to share in, enrich and be enriched by, the being of other things. In other words, we all recognize that intelligent being is better than unintelligent being; that a being able to give and receive love is better than one that cannot; that our way of being is better, richer and fuller than that of a stone, a flower, an earthworm, an ant, or even a baby seal.[22]

To say that there are degrees or gradations of "perfection" is to say that, ultimately, there are degrees of being.

But since these beings are finite, since they are not self-explanatory or self-sufficient, their being and, hence, what value they possess must ultimately derive from a maximum being, a being that is infinite, the source and condition of all value. This being Thomas says is God.

Dawkins' objection that either smelliness or "any" other "dimension of comparison" could be substituted for Thomas' "perfection," then, falls flat. Thomas's allusion to gradations of perfections is not arbitrary. Being, a perfection that is the ground of all other perfections, is inherently positive. Things like, say, evil, while real, are not beings per se but, rather, *defects* of being. They are deficiencies, corruptions of being.

Evil is like darkness, coldness, silence, and sickness, all of which are real, but whose reality is negative. Darkness is but the absence of light. Coldness, silence, and sickness are but absences

Christianity and the World

of heat, noise, and health. And evil is just a deprivation of the good.

So, to suggest, as Dawkins implies, that by Thomas's reasoning, gradations of, say, evil require that there be a maximum standard and source of evil is to both speak falsely and entirely misunderstand Thomas's position. There is no maximum standard and ground of evil, for the more evil a thing is the less being it possesses. Things are more evil the more goodness they lack. The more evil is something, the less reality, the more toward nonbeing it tends.

Thomas's fifth way is what he describes is a version of what's known as "the argument from design." He writes:

> We see that things which lack knowledge, such as natural bodies, act for an end, and this is evident from their acting always, or nearly always, in the same way, so as to obtain the best result. Hence it is plain that they achieve their end, not fortuitously, but designedly. Now whatever lacks knowledge cannot move towards an end, unless it be directed by some being endowed with knowledge and intelligence; as the arrow is directed by the archer. Therefore some intelligent being exists by whom all natural things are directed to their end; and this being we call God.

"Natural bodies"—things like planets, stars, plants, animals, i.e. things that are mindless, "which lack knowledge"—act *as if* they had minds because they behave in orderly or "designedly" ways. Since these mindless beings act mindfully, it can only be because they are being "directed" *by a mind,* a mind that Aquinas identifies with God.

In its bare bones, the argument from design boils down to this: The staggering complexity that we encounter throughout the natural world conveys the appearance that the universe has been designed. This means that it points beyond itself to a supreme intelligence that designed it.

Aquinas' was neither the first nor final version of the design argument. It certainly isn't among the stronger of its versions. Contra Dawkins, in our own time, especially since the discovery of DNA, the idea that the universe generally and life specifically are products of blind "evolutionary" processes is difficult to sustain.

Antony Flew is an English philosopher who practically revolutionized the field of philosophy of religion during the latter half of the 20th century. Yet he did so by posing a series of *challenges to theism*, for Flew was an atheist. Indeed, one would be hard pressed to think of any other philosopher who argued as rigorously, tirelessly, and for as long a period of time (over 50 years) against theism as did Flew. He was indeed the world's most renowned philosophical atheist for much of his professional existence. But in the early 2000s, about a dozen or so years ago, something happened: Flew announced to the world that his lifelong commitment to "follow the argument to wherever it leads" led him to *reject* his atheism.

Flew, near the end of his long life, came to believe that he had been wrong. As the title of the memoir within which he chronicles his intellectual odyssey from atheism to theism says, "There *is* a God." This is what Flew came to recognize. One of the arguments that convinced him of this is the design argument.

In addressing the laws of nature, Flew writes: "The important point is not merely that there are regularities in nature, but that these regularities are mathematically precise, universal, and 'tied together.'" "The question we should ask," Flew continues, "is how nature came packaged in this fashion." He notes that this is "the question that scientists from Newton to Einstein to Heisenberg have asked—and answered." Crucially: "Their answer was the Mind of God." [23]

Flew underscores that "many prominent scientists of the modern era have regarded the laws of nature" in this light,[24] and insinuates that Dawkins is dishonest in depicting Einstein, the most famous of 20th century scientists, as an atheist—a judgment that Flew himself once shared. Dawkins, Flew remarks, "ignores Einstein's categorical statement…that he was neither an atheist nor a pantheist."[25] He also ignores the comments of Max Jammer, a close friend of Einstein's and one who Dawkins has frequently cited on other matters, who expressly said that it made Einstein "angry" that atheists quoted him in support of their position.

Flew quotes from Jammer's *Einstein and Religion* in which the author expresses Einstein's position unequivocally: "Einstein always protested against being regarded as an atheist."[26]

It was at one of Flew's last public debates at a symposium at New York University in 2004 that he shocked his interlocutors and the audience as well with his announcement that he now believed in the existence of God. When, shortly afterwards, he was asked whether he thought that recent research into the origins of life supplied evidence for a Designer, Flew responded thus:

> *Yes, I now think it does…almost entirely because of the DNA investigations. What I think the DNA material has done is that it has shown, by the almost unbelievable complexity of the arrangements which are needed to produce (life), that intelligence must have been involved in getting these extraordinarily diverse elements to work together. It's the enormous complexity of the number of elements and the enormous subtlety of the ways they work together. The meeting of these two parts at the right time by chance is simply minute. It is all a matter of the enormous complexity by which the results were achieved, which looked to me like the work of intelligence.*[27]

Jack Kerwick

That the universe came about through chance is extremely remote indeed. During this event, an Israeli scientist, Gerald Schroeder, spoke alongside Flew. Schroeder dismembered what Flew describes as "the monkey theorem."

The "monkey theorem" is a species of the old argument—a claim, really, more than an argument—intended to show that, given a sufficiently lengthy period of time, the complex order that we see in the universe could and would emerge randomly from disorder. According to the analogy, if a group of monkeys was randomly pounding inexhaustibly on computer keys over a very long passage of time, eventually, they would be able to produce a Shakespearean sonnet. Schroeder, upon alluding to a British National Council of Arts study that involved a computer that was placed in a cage with six real monkeys for a month, proceeded to show that not only would our hypothetical monkeys never be able to produce a sonnet; *the universe* could never (randomly) produce a single Shakespearean sonnet (to say nothing of all of the other complex order of which it consists).

Schroeder selected one sonnet of Shakespeare's. Its opening line is, "Shall I compare thee to a summer's day?" The entire sonnet is comprised of 488 letters. He informs us that the "likelihood of hammering away and getting 488 letters in the exact sequence" as this opening line is "26 multiplied by itself 488 times—or 26 to the 488th power." This is equivalent to 10 to the 690th." The problem is that there aren't remotely enough particles in the whole universe to accommodate all of these trials. The total number of particles—protons, neutrons, and electrons—in the universe is 10 to the 80th, or one with 80 zeroes following it. Schroeder writes:

> *If you took the entire universe and converted it to computer chips—forget the monkeys—each one weighing a millionth of a gram and had each computer chip able to spin out 488 trials at, say, a million times*

> *a second; if you turn the entire universe into these microcomputer chips and these chips were spinning a million times a second [producing] random letters, the number of trials you would get since the beginning of time would be 10 to the 90th trials. It would be off again by a factor of 10 to the 600th. You will never get a sonnet by chance. The universe would have to be 10 to the 600th times larger.*

Schroeder adds, humorously: "Yet the world just thinks the monkeys can do it every time." [28]

In summary, it would take 10 to the 690th trials to randomly produce a Shakespearean sonnet. But given the total number of particles that it contains, the spatial-temporal universe only allows for 10 to the 90th trials.

Dawkins' assertions to the contrary aside, neither Charles Darwin nor anyone else ever put the design argument out to pasture. Just the opposite is true: Contemporary science reinforces (even if it doesn't necessarily prove) the design thesis.

To repeat, the point here is not to show that the historical "proofs" for God's existence necessarily succeed in fulfilling the task that they've been assigned. Rather, the point of the foregoing is twofold.

First, I wanted to show that there *are*, in fact, rational arguments for God's existence, i.e. arguments designed to establish the rational defensibility of theism. They admit of multiple versions that have been developed and vigorously defended over the span of many centuries by some of the keenest minds in the history of the world. Readers of such "new atheists" as Dawkins would never know any of this.

Second, precisely because of the wildly unjust treatment to which Dawkins and his ilk subject theism generally, and Christian theism specifically, it was imperative that the injustice be exposed. I trust that this goal was accomplished, that the reader now sees that Dawkins' case against the arguments for theism, relying as it does upon a battery of logical fallacies, fares no better than does Sam Harris' case for an a-theistic, objective morality.

CHAPTER IV

Christianity, the Most Persecuted of Religions

CHRISTIAN PERSECUTORS?! NO, Christian Victims!

On April 25, *USA Today* featured an article on its first page beneath a big, bold headline that read: "Gays face reversal of anti-bias protections."

This is but one more case of Fake News.

Fifty-one Republican lawmakers have implored President Trump to keep a campaign promise to restore the religious liberties of Americans that came under assault courtesy of his predecessor, Barack Obama. Among these is the liberty of non-profit groups like Catholic Charities, the largest charitable organization *in the world,* to adopt children to heterosexual couples only.

By the lights of the left, as exemplified by *USA Today,* Christians (and, by implication, anyone and everyone else) who think that, all things being equal, it is better for a child to be raised by a mother and a father rather than by two mommies or two daddies is guilty of "homophobia."

That Christians work tirelessly to spare the lives of the most vulnerable among us, the unborn, and provide them with families is of no consequence. As long as they insist upon placing these children exclusively in heterosexual-headed homes, they deserve to be morally condemned and legally punished for "discrimination."

If the owners of a small, family-run bakery are Christian, and if they refuse to bake a cake for a gay "wedding," the champions of "gay rights" besiege them with a tsunami of moral criticism and seek to bring the weight of government crashing down upon them.

It is no overstatement to say of Christians, or at least of those Christians who are determined to practice their faith in peace, that they do indeed meet with some degree of persecution or oppression in the America of 2017. Though Christians had been mocked for decades, the law was used against them during Obama's tenure in office when the former POTUS, via "Obamacare," required Catholic employers to subsidize abortion services and contraceptives for their employees.

And contrary to what the left would have us think, it is not Muslims and gays who suffer the greatest degree of persecution worldwide, but Christians who hold this distinction.

What Christians experience in America, while unjust, is of nothing compared to what their brothers and sisters in the faith are made to endure around the globe.

To note one recent and particularly grisly illustration of what Christians are up against, in Egypt, on Palm Sunday, two churches were bombed by Islamic militants at congregants who gathered to celebrate the first day of Holy Week. A minimum of 45 people were killed. According to Human Rights Watch, two parishioners and a pastor from one of the targeted houses of worship informed the organization that they suspected that some of the police that were supposed to be guarding the church allowed the terrorists to execute their murderous designs.

Christianity and the World

Human Rights Watch reports:

> In Tanta...a man wearing concealed explosives managed to pass through a security check outside St. George's Church and detonate himself near the front pews, killing at least 28 people and wounding 77 [.]

Meanwhile, in Alexandria, "church security camera footage showed another bomber trying to enter St. Mark's Church through an open gate and being directed toward a metal detector guarded by police officers. When an officer stopped the man, he detonated his explosives, killing at least 17 people and wounding 48."

Just 11 days before these attacks, police had to defuse a bomb that was arranged to be detonated right next to St. George's church. That the police were supposedly caught off guard by the Palm Sunday slaughter in spite of what had happened a week-and-a-half earlier is what led some to think that the officers may have been complicit in the bombings.

A pastor from one of the churches, a man who lost his son in the attack, stated bluntly that the church security that the government had provided was mere "decoration." "There's scenery," he said. "Just scenery."

Of course, Egypt is hardly unique in respect of the subject of the fierce persecution of Christians. According to Open Doors, an organization that serves persecuted Christians around the world, there are 20 countries in which Christians actually have it worse off than do their Egyptian brethren.

Of the Earth's 2 billion or so disciples of Christ, one in 12 is subject to "high," "very high," and "extreme" persecution for no other reason than that of their faith.

The Center for the Study of Global Christianity found that over a ten year period, from 2005 to 2015, about *90,000* Christians per year were killed for their commitment to Christ.

According to Open Doors, during the span of a mere one year period, from the end of October of 2015 to the beginning of November 2016, 1,207 Christians were martyred, i.e. murdered for their faith. The actual number is doubtless significantly higher, for statistics are difficult to come by when dealing with some of the planet's largest purveyors of anti-Christian oppression. North Korea, for instance, is ranked by Open Doors as the single most egregious violator of the rights of Christians—yet there is no formal statistical data documenting Christian casualties.

The same is true of regions of Iraq and Syria, two other bastions of anti-Christian oppression. (Iraq specifically has witnessed a precipitous decline in its ancient Christian population. In 2003, 1.5 million Christians resided in Iraq. At present, only about 275,000 remain.)

Between 2015 and 2016, 1,329 churches worldwide were attacked.

Eighty-percent of the world's most hostile climes for Christians—40 of 50—are found within Islamic-dominated lands.

Perhaps this goes some distance toward explaining why leftist agents of tolerance, like the folks at *USA Today,* spill little to no ink in covering this global phenomenon.

Or maybe it's simply that they lack empathy for Christians, i.e. those who they suspect may "discriminate" against gays by refusing to enthusiastically embrace "gay marriage."

"Islamophobia" in America vs. Murderous Christophobia in the Islamic World

As organizations like CAIR and their allies wax indignant over "Islamophobia" in America, Muslims around the globe are visiting the worst sort of cruelty upon the Christian minorities in their midst.

For instance, over a span of four days, from October 19-23, the Indonesian government succumbed to the demand of Islamic "extremists" and demolished nine churches. Six days earlier, on October 13, Muslims unleashed a torrent of violence that left a church burned to the ground and a person dead.

And in the course of this single day, *8,000* Christians found themselves displaced from their homes.

The government has deported them.

According to a local church activist, someone who self-identified only as "Rudy," Islamic militants issued an ultimatum to the Indonesian government: Either raze these Christian churches to the ground or "the radicals will deploy around 7,000 people" to besiege this Christian community.

The organization Open Doors, a group dedicated to "serving persecuted Christians worldwide," reports: "Church members wept as they watched in despair [as] civil police officers [began] hammering down their worship houses." As of this juncture, over 1,000 "churchless believers are prohibited from raising temporary tents to hold Sunday worship services."

The predominantly Islamic country of Bangladesh is a place where Christian women are regularly subjected to unspeakable violence. Open Doors states that "two out of every three women in Bangladesh will experience gender-based violence in their lifetimes." Furthermore, the United Nations' "Special Rapporteur on Violence Against Women" has found that "girls are regularly harassed and abused on their way to and from school," a phenomenon that is the function of the fact that "sexual harassment is often seen as 'part of the culture.'"

One young woman who has fallen victim to this culture is Susmita Chambugonj. Back in May, the 20 year-old was assailed by five "youths" who dragged her into a microbus. While inside, Susmita was raped by two of her abductors.

The current "refugee crisis" has hit Syrian and Iraqi Christians particularly hard. Open Doors informs us that Christians in these countries "have had their homes marked by ISIS," and "some come from historically Christian towns that were obliterated." Moreover, some Christians are discovering "that they are being discriminated against when it comes to receiving aid."

In Africa, stories of Islamic-on-Christian oppression are even more grisly. At the same time, these same stories supply us with proverbial textbook exhibitions of Christian heroism.

Earlier in the year Boko Haram paid Habila Adamu a visit at his home. When the militants informed Habila that they were "looking for him" in order to end his life, he replied that he had been looking for them as well—but in order to share with them the Gospel of Christ.

The predators weren't impressed. When Habila refused to recant his faith, his persecutors shot him in the face and left him for dead.

Thankfully, Habila survived.

Joshua, however, did not.

Joshua was 18 years old. A member of a family of farmers, he worked in a factory during the dry season. One day, Islamic militants showed up at his place of employment and proceeded to separate those employees who were Muslims from those that were Christians. Then, they wasted no time in murdering the Christians one by one.

Initially, Joshua was in another room with some other employees. They watched through a window as the mass murder unfolded. When an Islamic woman and fellow employee of Joshua begged the latter to deny his Christianity, he refused. Joshua was blunt: "No," he told her, for "I am a Christian and they are killing my brothers."

Joshua continued: "I am also going out there. I am not going to stay here and pretend that I am a Muslim."

Joshua was martyred along with nine young men.

Even as I write this, the Christian community in Turkey is the object of a systematic, relentless campaign of death threats. According to Open Doors, the targeted were blasted for being "heretics" who have "chosen the path that denies Allah [.]"

In Pakistan this past July, Saddique Azam, a veteran school teacher, was promoted to the position of "headmaster" at an elementary school. Azam is a Christian. For months, he was repeatedly threatened by Muslims who believed that the office of headmaster should be held by a Muslim. Azam refused to resign.

Then, on October 6, three of his Islamic colleagues who worked under him physically attacked Azam.

Azam recounted his experience: "Three Muslim teachers entered the school, went into my office and waited for me there. When I entered the office, I was alarmed to see them. I asked them the reason for the visit and they launched a tirade of warnings against me to withdraw and resign from teacher headship."

From the beating, Azam sustained a severe injury to his left eye. Things could've been worst had it not been for other staff that stopped the assault.

But witnesses reported that while they pummeled Azam, his Islamic assailants mocked him by referring to him as "choora," an anti-Christian epithet used by Pakistani Muslims. "Choora" connotes the "sweeper" or "untouchable" caste. "You are a 'Christian Choora,'" his victimizers shouted. How, then, "can you be a headmaster and be given seniority over us?"

The next time that we hear about the "Islamophobia" that Muslims in America allegedly face, let's recall the face of real religious persecution: the persecution that truly defenseless Christians suffer at the hands of Muslim aggressors throughout the Islamic world.

Jack Kerwick

Which is the Real Problem, "Islamophobia" or Christophobia?

"Islamophobia" is a *real* problem.

Or so we're led to believe by the usual suspects in the grievance industry par excellence, the Racism-Industrial-Complex (RIC).

It's a problem because, it is tirelessly declared, "Islamophobia" is only going to create more Islamic "extremists."

An article from a December 2015 edition of *The Independent* represents this all too common view. The title of the piece reads: "Want to create more extremists? Ignore the Islamophobia people like me face every day." The author is Shehab Khan, a Muslim who lives in England.

Khan opens his editorial by relaying a story. Supposedly, an 11 year-old boy and the child of one his friends was the only one of his peers to have not been invited to a classmate's birthday party. The reason, according to Khan, is that the parents of the birthday child expressly said that they didn't want any Muslims to attend the party, for it was Muslims who were responsible for "7/7," the London bombings on July 7, 2005 that took the lives of 52 people and injured over 700 more.

Khan continues, stating that, "as a Muslim myself, I face similar prejudice every day [.]" He is more direct: "Violence and aggression motivated by Islamophobia has, unfortunately, become almost routine."

However, "arguably the biggest issue is the clear and persistent presence of institutional Islamophobia."

"Islamophobia," Khan says, "is endemic and insidious in almost all sections of society and doesn't just occur when people's smartphones are on and the headlines are made."

But here Khan delivers his ultimate point: If the biggest threat the West faces today stems from such Islamic terrorist organizations as ISIS, then "Islamophobia" is a genuine crisis, an issue of national security in every one of those countries that comprise Western civilization. Why? Khan elaborates:

"Continually singling out Muslims and questioning them about affiliations with Isis and whether they are extremists is a personification of Islamophobia. Institutional or casual, Islamophobia not only affects British Muslims but also plays into the narrative put forward by extremists that the west will never accept Muslims."

He concludes: "If we want successful counter-terrorism policy, we need to start with tackling the racism which plays into the terrorist narrative. We ignore prejudice at our own peril."

Notice, the "terrorist narrative" to which Khan alludes is *his* narrative, the tale of talking points that RIC agents promote at every turn. Let's call it "the Islamophobia narrative."

First, there is the assumption that "Islamophobia" is a meaningful term.

Second, we have the assertion, always presented as axiomatic, that Islamophobia is at once pervasive and oppressive.

Third, the case for this last typically depends, as it depends here, on unverifiable anecdotes of the kind that Khan shares, stories of Muslims who felt as if they had been slighted or inconvenienced because of their religion.

Finally, the Islamophobia narrative, like that of the "terrorist narrative" (at least as Khan understands the latter), insists in so many words that unless Westerners refrain from lending offense to those Muslims that they have allowed into their lands, they will pay for it with their own blood.

Islamophobia, you see, is guaranteed to fuel terrorism.

Interestingly, but unsurprisingly, the Khans of the world never utter a peep about "*Christ*ophobia," the oppression, the often brutal oppression, to which Christians around the world are subjected on a daily basis. Nor are they willing to mention that much (though certainly not all) of this anti-Christian cruelty is perpetrated by Muslims in majority-Muslim societies.

There are 44 Muslim-majority countries in the world comprised of a total of 1.1 billion practitioners of Islam. In 38 of these countries, Christians constitute the single largest religious minority. About 56 million, or 2.6%, of the people living in these 44 countries are Christian.

There are degrees of persecution that Christians face, it's true, but as immediately becomes obvious to any unprejudiced observer, the examples that Westerners like Khan offer as proof of anti-Muslim oppression are outright embarrassing when compared to those that Christians can and have provided of the treatment to which they are prey.

If it's true that an 11 year-old Muslim child was excluded from a classmate's party just because of his religion, this is indeed sad. But when it is considered in juxtaposition with the fact that over the span of a decade, from 2005 to 2015, militant Muslims reduced the ancient Christian community in Iraq from 1.5 million residents to 300,000, and over half of the latter have been displaced from their homes, things don't sound like their all that rough for Muslims in historically Christian countries.

If it's true that innocent Muslims in, say, England have been questioned by authorities on the basis of their religion alone about possible connections with terrorist groups, and they were inconvenienced by this, then while this may be unfortunate, it hardly screams of oppression when it is contrasted with ISIS armies chasing tens of thousands of Christian families from their homes.

One study suggests that Christians are facing genocidal conditions of an enormity such that by 2020 or so, Christians will have been cleansed from much of the Middle East, a region in which they've resided for two millennia.

And yet, no one who has dared to note any of this ugliness has ever so much as remotely suggested that the persecution of Christians should stop because it will fuel Christian terrorism.

If we insist on talking about "Islamophobia," then we have no option but to admit that it stands as a cold to the stage five cancer of Christophobia.

Muslim Murderers, Christian Victims in Nigeria

As the self-appointed guardians of all that is virtuous and just incessantly berate as "Islamophobic" those of their compatriots who entertain second thoughts about importing Islamic culture into the West, these same self-avowed agents of "tolerance" utter not a peep regarding the murderous persecution to which Christians and other religious minorities are daily subjected throughout the Islamic world (and beyond).

Voice of the Martyrs (VOM) is one organization that exists to raise awareness of this crisis.

In at least 50 countries around the globe, Christians suffer "severe" oppression. Most of these countries—about 80%--have near exclusively Muslim majority populations.

Take, for example, "Amina." Amina is a Nigerian woman who, in 2011, was staying with her friend "Charity" and the latter's children when their village was besieged by Islamic militants firing guns.

Charity was ill and Amina was nearly seven months pregnant when the militants began raining down gunfire. Since their home was surrounded by a "high wall," the women lead the children out of the house toward the back and helped them climb over it. Unfortunately, however, given their own respective conditions, neither Charity nor Amina were capable of climbing the wall themselves.

"I was six months then, going on seven, and my stomach was big," Amina recalls. She proceeded to search out a room in which to hide when she took a bullet to her leg.

Her sick friend dragged Amina into the house and found her a hiding space before finding one herself.

Yet to no avail. Amina's gun wound left a trail of blood that her Muslim assailants were able to track easily enough once they overcame the compound. Kicking in the door to the room in which she was hiding, they began to attack poor Amina with....*machetes.*

They attacked her with machetes.

Let this sink in: American leftists are apoplectic over the prospect of halting Islamic immigration to the United States, say, or—God forbid!—the expectation that "moderate" Muslims should denounce Islamic terror.

In glaring contrast, these same social justice warriors say nothing about the phenomenon of pregnant Christian women being awaken in the dead of night and butchered by machete and gun-wielding Muslim men.

Amina's tormentors didn't finish her off. They left her for dead and proceeded to rampage through the rest of the village. Charity found Amina in a pool of her own blood and tried to get her medical attention.

The problem, though, is that the motorbikes in the town had been destroyed by the marauders. Thankfully, however, Charity prevailed upon a Nigerian army patrol that transported Amina to a hospital.

Amina survived, and after *four months,* she was finally able to leave the hospital. Yet because of the immense blood loss that she suffered, she lost the baby that she had been carrying. Also, such was the severity of the injuries that she sustained that Amina to this day is incapable of walking properly.

Thus, she is unable to lend her husband and their family the financial assistance that she would've otherwise provided.

Christianity and the World

To make matters even worse, Amina's family home and all of their possessions were destroyed in a fire ignited by their Muslim oppressors.

Amina expresses her gratitude to Voice of the Martyrs for furnishing her and her family with the funds that they've needed for her to get the treatment and provisions that she needed to recover from her attack.

Remarkably—but both unsurprisingly and *uncommon* for devout Christians like Amina who have lost virtually all to monsters who target them because of their faith—Amina has *forgiven* her oppressors. "I don't have any bad intention against them," she remarks. "Our prayer is that they should understand that what they are doing is not good [.]" She insists that she has "forgiven them" and expresses hope "that they will be saved [.]"

Notice: Neither Amina nor her family nor Charity nor, for that matter, *any other Christian* that has suffered so senselessly in theses bastions of virulent Islamic persecution declaims their persecutors as "infidels," much less calls for their deaths.

Instead, they try to forgive them. And Amina, for her part, also admits to praying regularly "that in all of this suffering that I am passing through" God "will give me courage" to withstand anything "that…will tempt me to turn back from Him."

Amina's forgiveness, though, shouldn't be interpreted as passivity. She is adamant when she claims that her and her fellow oppressed Christians in Nigeria "want the world to know that Christians in norther Nigeria are passing through persecution." Muslims, she continues, "go and pick weapons and they hunt us in the night to take our lives, and they do all [these] things *because of the name of Jesus*."

Amina concludes: "If we agree to become Muslims they will let us be, but because they see that we refuse, they keep on hunting us."

As I document in my book, *The American Offensive: Dispatches from the Front* (Stairway Press), Amina's experience is all too common.

But all the left can talk about is "Islamophobia" in America.

Christophobia from a Global Perspective

Interesting times these are.

While the Pope of my church seems to spare no occasion to castigate Western societies for allegedly not doing enough to welcome and accommodate Islamic refugees from the Middle East, he rarely says anything about the epidemic of anti-Christian persecution around the world.

In stark contrast, while addressing the topic of Middle Easterners who are seeking refuge in the United States, President Trump—who, readers may recall, Pope Francis once suggested wasn't really a Christian because of his expressed desire to build a wall along America's southern border—explicitly resolved to provide relief for *Christians*.

Trump's critics immediately pounced on him for religious discrimination.

Some context on this matter readily reveals that the Pope's view is as morally confused as the President's is sensible.

Firstly, contrary to what the Christophobes would have us believe, Christianity is the most persecuted religion in the world today. In 2016, approximately 900,000 Christians suffered persecution.

Secondly, many (though not all) of these victimized Christians to whom the President was referring, those seeking refuge from the oppression that they've encountered in places like Syria, say, are prey to *Islamic* predators.

Of course it's true that there are decent Muslims (and others) who are also victimized by their co-religionists. Equally true, however, is that it *is* predominately Muslims who are menacing the vulnerable.

And they are menacing Christians because the latter reject the religion of Muhammad.

Yet it would be a mistake to think that it is *only* Muslims who persecute Christians.

Open Doors (OD) is among the organizations that exists for the sake of drawing people's attention to the phenomenon of anti-Christian persecution around the planet. It defines "persecution" thus:

> *Christian persecution is any hostility experienced from the world as a result of one's identification as a Christian. From verbal harassment to hostile feelings, attitudes and actions, Christians in areas of with severe religious restrictions pay a heavy price for their faith. Beatings, physical torture, confinement, isolation, rape, severe punishment, imprisonment, slavery, discrimination in education and employment, and even death are just a few examples of the persecution they experience on a daily basis.*

Christians in at least 60 countries suffer persecution because of their faith. On a monthly basis, 322 Christians are murdered. When they aren't losing their lives, 772 acts of violence—from rapes to beatings; from abductions to arrests and forced marriages—are visited upon them. And each month, 214 churches and Christian properties are destroyed.

Open Doors distinguishes three gradations of persecution: "extreme persecution," "very high persecution," and "high persecution." Of the 50 most oppressive countries for Christians, about four out of five them, or 80%, are Islamic.

However, the worse of the worst persecutors is North Korea.

North Korea's government is that of a communist dictatorship. Of its 25,405,000 residents, some 300,000 are Christian. The reasons cited by OD for the government's ruthless persecution of Christians are two: "communist oppression" and "dictatorial paranoia."

North Korea is a "totalitarian communist state" where "Christians are forced to hide their faith completely from government authorities, neighbors, and, often, even their own spouses and children." Because of the government's "ever-present surveillance, many pray with their eyes open, and gathering for praise or fellowship is practically impossible."

All North Koreans must worship the ruling family, "and those who don't comply (including Christians) are arrested, imprisoned, tortured or killed." Moreover, whole "Christian families are" routinely "imprisoned in hard labor camps, where unknown numbers die each year from torture, beatings, overexertion and starvation."

As for those who attempt to flee to South Korea via China, they "risk execution or life imprisonment [.]"

In North Korea, the act of possessing a Bible is a capital crime. Christians must meet secretly in the woods if they wish to worship.

In Islamic Nigeria, particularly the Borno State in the northeaster section of the country, there are 27 camps of roughly 5,000 "internally displaced peoples." The mostly Christian residents of these camps are infected with HIV/AIDS courtesy of the notorious Islamic terrorist organization Boko Haram, for most of the patients were once held captive by the latter.

The Boko Haram insurgency that transpired in Nigeria also decimated the Christian communities that had at one time existed there. Those Christians who returned to their homes are now in danger of starving, for there is no work, and those who did have work before they fled because of the insurgency have been fired from their jobs. Thus, they are under immense pressure from Muslims to convert to Islam in exchange for financial support.

And what about Iraq, a place that Christians had been calling home for as long as there have been Christians? Barack Obama's announcement to the world that he would be withdrawing troops from Iraq was the beginning of the end for the country's Christians, for the vacuum that he created in effect created the ruthless Islamic State (ISIS).

Iraq is the seventh most oppressive place on the planet for Christians. As OD states, although the Christian community in Iraq is ancient, it is now "on the verge of extinction." The Christian-aid organization elaborates:

> *The overall persecution situation in Iraq is characterized by impunity, the threat of attacks and second class treatment by the authorities. Historical Christian communities and Protestant Christian communities are seriously affected by persecution, especially from Islamic movements, authorities and non-Christian leaders. Communities of converts to Christianity from Islam suffer severely from persecution, especially at the hands of family, but also from the above mentioned persecutors if their faith is known.*

For all of the left's crocodile tears over "Islamophobia," Muslims are by far the least persecuted religious group in the world, and certainly throughout the Western world where they live far freer and better than they ever could have imagined doing in their homelands.

It is Christians who are under attack for their faith.

Jack Kerwick

Bringing Ramadan in with a Bang: Killing Christians in Egypt

Jeremy Joseph Christian is a 35 year-old white man who, according to some press reports, is also a "white supremacist."

Christian, you see, while aboard a train in Portland, Oregon, allegedly hurled "ethnic and religious" slurs at two young women who, evidently, appeared to have been Muslim. "Get off the bus and get out of the country because you don't pay taxes here," Christian is reported to have said. He also, supposedly, expressed a dislike for Muslims and characterized them as "criminals."

Three men who are now being hailed as "heroes" intervened. Christian killed two of them, slashing their throats. The third man was stabbed as well, but survived and is being treated for non-life threatening injuries.

There is much to this story that is still unclear (more will be written at a future time). Predictably, the Islamic activists of the Council on American-Islamic Relations (CAIR) spared not a moment to exploit this tragedy for their partisan purposes. CAIR's National Executive Director, Nihad Awad, expressly implicated President Trump: "President Trump must speak out personally against the rising tide of Islamophobia and other forms of bigotry and racism in our nation that he has provoked through his numerous statements, policies and appointments that have negatively impacted minority communities."

Awad's remarks are not only fundamentally untrue. For more than one reason, they are profoundly offensive.

One reason that they are offensive is that Muslims, far from being the most persecuted of religious groups in today's world, are in reality the biggest persecutors.

The reality is that if there is a "rising tide" of any species of violent bigotry, it is *Christophobia,* not Islamophobia. No religion is as persecuted around the planet as that of Christianity.

Christianity and the World

In February, the Center for Studies on New Religions released a study showing that last year, 90,000 Christians throughout the world were murdered because of their faith. Nearly one-third of these victims were killed by Muslims. According to Open Doors, an advocacy organization for persecuted Christians, 14 of the 20 worst purveyors of Christian persecution are Islamic countries, and the latter constitute 35 of the worst 50.

Middle Eastern wars in places like Yemen, Syria, and Iraq have been particularly hard on the ancient Christian communities that exist among the Islamic majorities. Legions of men, women, and children have been slaughtered, maimed, and/or displaced.

Yet the world utters virtually a peep. Pope Francis, for example, the Pope of my church, while he has indeed commented here and there on the oppression of Christians, he may as well have said nothing, for the Pope's remarks on this matter have been like whispers relative to the pleas that he makes incessantly on behalf of Islamic refugees.

And while the leftist media in the West seeks to establish a connection between the beginning of Ramadan and Jeremy Christian's *insulting* of two Islamic women, over in Egypt some Muslims inaugurated the holy month by...*slaughtering* dozens of Christian men, women, and children.

The most recent outrage committed against Christians occurred on May 26 in Egypt. Islamic terrorists attacked a bus full of Coptic Christians, murdering 28 and injuring many more. Children were among the victims.

The victims were reportedly heading to St. Samuel the Confessor monastery when their bus was blocked by three vehicles and eight to ten assailants wearing military uniforms and masks. The attackers proceeded to blast gunfire into the bus.

The so-called "Islamic State" (ISIS) claimed "credit" for the bloodbath.

In what now reads as ominously as it does presciently, an article published but two days before this attack at the website of *Open Doors* and authored by one of its Egyptian staff members speaks to the fever-pitch anxieties that the impending Islamic holiday of Ramadan have induced in the members of Egypt's Christian community. It is worth reading "Janelle P" in her own words:

> *As much excitement as the Islamic holy month brings to Muslims, it does carry a great deal of burdens and concerns to the Christian community in Egypt. It is a very long 30 days during which Christians in schools, work or public spaces will receive harsh looks and verbal harassments from devout Muslims because of their faith. They are ridiculed for not fasting like Muslims. Even in some cases, Christians may face physical violence due to the fact that they were caught eating their lunch by their fasting Muslim coworkers or neighbors!*

Think about this: Due to the celebration of an Islamic holiday, Christians have to brave insults, hostility, and even physical violence.

Janelle P continues: "It's not uncommon for Christians to hide somewhere to eat their lunches away from the eyes of the Muslims." Janelle recalls his own experiences growing up in Egypt. "I remember as a young boy having to eat and drink in the school toilet to avoid trouble with Muslim classmates and teachers."

Young Christian children must take shelter in school restrooms if they want to eat their lunch unmolested by their Islamic classmates.

> *It's almost protocol during the month of Ramadan for devout Muslims, wherever they are, to turn to the*

> *Christians around them and bombard them with intimidating questions about their faith. They aim to distract themselves from the long fasting hours and, if they're lucky enough, to plant doubt in the hearts of the Christians.*

Janelle P concludes by acknowledging that "We, the Christians of Egypt, feel many different emotions regarding Ramadan." However, he presumably speaks for his coreligionists in Egypt when Janelle expresses, not rage or hatred, but rather *faith* that God will show Muslims the error of their ways and bring them to Him. It is this, at any rate, for which they pray.

The attitude of love that the most oppressed Christians hold toward their Islamic oppressors stands in glaring contrast to that which Muslims have toward those who do not share their vision.

Of course, the point here is not to suggest that all of the world's billion or so Muslims deserve to be condemned for the actions of the exploitative, oppressive, and murderous among them. Such a suggestion is unwarranted. Nor would it be right to suggest that no Muslims experience persecution. There are indeed persecuted Muslims throughout the world, but the persecution that they suffer is almost without exception at the hands of other Muslims.

The point of this essay is to puncture the West's Politically Correct meme, an ideologically-useful fiction according to which Muslims are always victims and Christians are victimizers—or, at the very least, are never victimized.

The painful reality is that, globally speaking, when it comes to the topic of religious persecution, the adherents of Islam are the biggest persecutors while those of Christianity are victimized more so than the members of any other religious faith.

Jack Kerwick

Suffering Christians in Nigeria

Roman Catholics throughout the world are in the midst of the season of Lent.

Lent occurs over the six weeks stretching between Ash Wednesday and Easter Sunday. It is recognized by Catholics as a season of renewal, a time for Christians to repent of their sins and draw nearer to God.

And while prayer is essential to renewing one's relationship with one's Creator, Sustainer, and Savior, unless prayer is accompanied by the love of one's neighbors, it is in vain.

There are two things that every Christian knows: (1) The love of neighbor transcends any and every boundary that human weakness—human sin—disposes us to draw; and (2) This *agape* (highest form of love) can be expressed in any number of ways.

These facts considered, Christians in America—particularly during this Holy Season—should bear in mind the plight of their brothers and sisters in the faith around the globe who are made daily to endure persecution of a kind that few of us can scarcely conceive.

The victims are men, women, and children to whom we are now and probably always will be strangers. They are almost always people of color, not infrequently (but by no stretch invariably) Africans and Middle Easterners.

And most (but not all) of the time, their persecutors are *Muslims*.

As black multimillionaires boycott *the Oscars* for Hollywood's failure to nominate blacks for this most prestigious of its awards; as black and white agitators in the "Black Lives Matter" movement and among the Democrat Party's presidential candidates continue to bemoan "systemic 'racism'" in America; as the History Channel remakes the plagiarist Alex Haley's *Roots;* and as Islamic activists bemoan such "Islamophobic" policies as "profiling" passengers boarding airplanes, black African Christians are regularly enslaved, beaten, separated from their families and murdered—usually by African Muslims.

Yet not a peep do we hear from Westerners who decry "racism" and religious bigotry as the most egregious of evils.

Open Doors, a site committed to serving oppressed Christians wherever they may be, shares stories of the victims of the Islamic militant group Boko Haram. The latter has been especially cancerous for the residents of Nigeria.

In April of 2014, the world watched as Michele Obama launched her "hashtag" campaign against Boko Haram when the thugs abducted 276 school girls from their secondary school in Chibok in Borno State. Chibok is an essentially Christian village. On May 5, less than one month after the kidnappings, Boko Haram's leader, Abubakar Shekau, made a video in which he acknowledged that the girls were targeted precisely because they were *not* Christian: "The girls that have not accepted Islam, they are now gathered in numbers" but "treated...well the way the Prophet Muhammad treated the infidels he seized."

He added: "Slavery is allowed in my religion, and I shall capture people and make them slaves."

The girls shouldn't have been in school to begin with, Shekau insisted, for as long as they are at least nine years of age, they are suitable for marriage.

Open Doors has touched base with the father of one of the Chibok girls. The man's name is James. James' "heart aches every day" for his daughter, yet he continues to pray for her safe return.

Lydia survived one of the random bomb attacks that Boko Haram launched in Gobe State (Nigeria). Open Doors assures us that, "miraculously, amidst such a nightmare, she still has sure hope in the Lord."

There's also Esther. Open Doors reports: "At the hands of Boko Haram, she has now become a widow. Her husband would not deny Jesus, even to the point of death, and that brings her joy when her mourning is overwhelming."

Things have only gotten worse for these beleaguered people.

In just one year, from 2014-2015, the rate of Muslim-on-Christian murder has risen by *62 percent* in Nigeria. In 2014, Open Doors recorded 2,484 murders and 108 attacks on churches. In 2015, however, it determined that there were at least *4,028 murders* and *198* church attacks.

Open Doors joined with the Christian Association of Nigeria (CAN) to conduct a report on the violence. According to "a partner director for West Africa," the report—"Crushed but not defeated, the impact of persistent violence on the church in northern Nigeria"—reveals that "the extent and impact of the persistent violence on the church…is much more serious than previously expected."

This may come as a surprise to Westerners who would love to believe that only a small handful of aberrant or heterodox Muslims—"extremists," as Barack Obama calls them—is responsible for the infamous violence perpetrated in the name of Allah, but this report also notes that even if *Boko Haram was destroyed tomorrow*, the threat to Christians would *persist*.

For starters, the 30 million or so Christians in the region "have suffered marginalization and discrimination as well as targeted violence" for several decades: This oppression wasn't born with the relatively recent rise of Boko Haram.

Nor will it end with the ending of the terrorist outfit. "Once Boko Haram is defeated," comments the West African partner director (who, for obvious reasons, wished to remain anonymous), "the problem will not be solved." The director explains: "Christians living under Sharia law are facing discrimination and marginalization and have limited to no access to federal rights."

The report on the persecution of the northern Nigerian church identifies three principal sources of the epidemic to which it speaks—and Boko Haram is only *one* of them. The other two are the Muslim Fulani herdsmen and "the Muslim religious and political elite that dominates government in norther Nigeria."

This Lenten season, and every season, as the racial and religious-grievance mongers of the Racism-Industrial-Complex here at home seek out increasingly incredible instances of bigotry, Christians and all decent people should muster the courage to speak for real victims of evil.

Some of those real victims are Christian men, women, and children in places like Nigeria.

Christian Persecution at Home

The phenomenally successful restaurant franchise Chick-Fil-A is once again at the center of national controversy. And, once again, it is a controversy generated by those who waste not a moment to equate opposition to so-called "same sex marriage" with "hate."

A couple of weeks ago, Chick-Fil-A's CEO, Dan Cathy, told Online Baptist Press that his restaurant was committed to advancing the well-being of "the family—the biblical definition of the family unit." He continued: "We are a family-owned business, a family-led business, and we are married to our first wives." For this, Cathy said that he gives "God thanks [.]"

He also mentioned that he prays that we are not "inviting God's judgment on our nation when we shake our fist at him and say, 'We know better than you as to what constitutes a marriage.'" Such an attitude, Cathy asserts, is unduly "prideful" and "arrogant."

In response to Cathy's remarks, mayors from American's metropolises have "disinvited" Chick-Fil-A from opening any new restaurants in their cities. For example, former White House Chief of Staff to Barack Obama and current Chicago Mayor Rahm

Emanuel stated: " Chick-Fil-A's values are not Chicago's values. They [Chick-Fil-A] disrespect our fellow neighbors and residents."

Considering that Chicago has been a killing field under his watch, Mayor Emanuel's remarks may very well have done more than anything else could have to help make Chick-Fil-A even more successful than it already is.

In all seriousness, though, we need to really observe what is happening here.

As Dan Cathy says, Chick-Fil-A is a *family*-owned business. More specifically, it is a *Christian* family-owned business. And although he is reluctant to characterize his business in terms of Christianity—only individuals can have a relationship with Christ, corporations can't—the fact of the matter is that Chick-Fil-A is designed to resolutely affirm what can only be described as Christian values.

The most salient of such signs is its decision to do business only six days of every week: every Sunday Chick-Fil-A is closed.

But it also routinely—incessantly—sponsors all manner of family-friendly events, and donates substantial sums of money to the most deserving of charities.

In short, Chick-Fil-A most definitely *is* a Christian organization.

This is why it continually comes under attack by those who are determined to insure that the voice of anything that can remotely be construed as a traditional form of Christianity is silenced. Cathy's latest comments are but a pretext for what amounts to nothing more or less than a relentless campaign by radical leftist forces to relegate the Christian to the periphery of the culture.

If we think about it for more than the length of a standard sound bite, we will discover that this verdict is inescapable.

Think about what Cathy is *not* saying. He is *not* saying that Chick-Fil-A refuses to serve homosexuals. He is *not* even saying that his business would refuse to *hire* homosexuals. He hasn't said anything even close to this.

Chick-Fil-A does indeed engage in discriminatory hiring practices. Yet there is one simple criterion that it employs, and it hasn't a thing to do with sexuality (or race, gender, etc.).

Being a dutiful Chick-Fil-A customer, I have gotten to know some of its managers over the last so many years, and they have all told me the same thing: all members of the Chick-Fil-A staff must be able to provide excellent customer service.

What this in turn means is that they must not only be *efficient* in providing customers with the goods that they purchase; they must do so with a smile.

In other words, applicants must either possess a cheery disposition at the time of being hired, or they must possess the will to acquire such a disposition during on-the-job training.

In terms of hospitality, there is no fast food restaurant on the planet quite like Chick-Fil-A. To this, everyone who has ever eaten there, regardless of their opinion regarding the quality of its food, can readily attest.

Chick-Fil-A supplies people—its customers, its employees, and untold legions of human beings who have been the beneficiaries of its charitable activities—a service that is immeasurable in worth. Without exaggeration, it can be said that Chick-Fil-A has gone a great distance in helping the lives that it has touched achieve what, as Aristotle long ago recognized, all of us ultimately want: happiness.

Chick-Fil-A is a character molding institution insofar as it aspires to cultivate within its employees those habits that have traditionally been recognized as human *excellences* or *virtues*. The staff at the organization that the Cathy family founded promotes diligence, conscientiousness, humility, generosity, and hospitality.

And it even encourages—by way of its observance of the Christian Sabbath and the innumerable events that it sponsors on behalf of families and local communities—the *theological* virtues of faith, hope, and charity.

This is the organization that Chick-Fil-A's enemies relentlessly smear as a promoter of "hate." We must be clear, for clarity concerning the nature of Chick-Fil-A provides us in spades with clarity concerning the nature of its nemeses.

That the campaign against Chick-Fil-A is part and parcel of a much wider campaign against traditional Christianity becomes obvious once we consider that Cathy's position on so-called "same sex marriage" is no different than that taken by *the entire world* up until yesterday, as far as history is measured. Even our "transformative" President, that "world-historical," "multi-cultural" figure himself, Barack Obama, subscribed, or claimed to subscribe, to the same exact position as Cathy's up until just a couple of months ago.

Here is what we must grasp: if Cathy is "homophobic" because he does not support "gay marriage" or even homosexual activity, then what his enemies are actually charging is that traditional Christianity, from biblical days up until just a few decades ago, is "homophobic."

More simply put, the God of the Bible is a moral degenerate, for the God that is depicted from Genesis through Revelations is an unreconstructed "homophobe."

If Cathy and most of the two billion people who constitute the Christian world are "homophobes," it is because the God who they aspire to honor was a "homophobe" first.

Admittedly, no text or tradition is self-interpreting. Cathy and those of his theological ilk—i.e. most of his contemporaries and *all* of his predecessors of the last couple of millennia—may be mistaken in how they read Christianity. But if this is so, then it is incumbent upon his critics to point out to him the error of his ways.

This they haven't done.

Yet even if they could prove that Cathy and the overwhelming majority of human beings who have ever lived were incorrect, this would most definitely *not* justify the allegations of "hatred" and "homophobia" that Chick-Fil-A's enemies insist on substituting for rational and civil argument.

Christian Response to Anti-Christian Bullying

On August 1, legions of Americans from across the country came out in defense of Chick-Fil-A, the fabulously successful fast food chain that became the object of left-wing hostility when its owner and CEO, Dan Cathy, expressed his opposition to same sex marriage.

However, not everyone who sought out the nearest Chick-Fil-A restaurant intended to support it.

In Tucson, Arizona, a man named Adam Smith videotaped himself berating a 26 year-old Chick-Fil-A female employee named "Rachel."

But before he actually spoke to the woman, Smith recorded himself as saying: "People have to have to their Chick-Fil-A anti-gay breakfast sandwich." He added that it "always tastes better when it's full of hate."

When he arrived at the window, he informed the unsuspecting employee that her place of employment was a "hateful organization." She in turn explained that the Christian-based organization aspires to treat all of its customers well.

Yet Smith continued with his anti- Chick-Fil-A tirade, insisting that it supplies "money to hate groups"—i.e. groups that reject the notion that marriage should be radically rearranged to accommodate homosexuals.

As the employee handed Smith his beverage—a cup of water that is free of charge—she refused to compromise Chick-Fil-A's commitment to quality customer service. "It's my pleasure to serve you always," she stated.

Smith's wrath did not abate. "Of course I'm glad that I can take a little money from Chick-Fil-A and maybe less money to hate groups," he replied. "I don't know how you can live with yourself and work here. I don't understand it. This is a horrible corporation with horrible values."

When the employee bid Smith to have himself a "nice day," he assured her that he would, for he had just done "something purposeful." He explained, as he drove off, that he was "a nice guy [.]" Then he added that he was a heterosexual that "just can't stand the hate [.]"

Smith's video went viral. But it was met with largely negative responses.

"Hey that's great," wrote one Facebook poster, "hassle some poor slob in a menial position trying to make ends meet at the drive through window. Way to go Adam, you really 'did something purposeful' there, you jackass."

Another person said: "We need to know where this person works and flood the company with phone calls and email demanding that he be fired."

One person commented: "Talk about a major case of backfire, LOL…stories like these continue to show who the real haters are."

Even those who agree with Smith's cause acknowledged that he was in the wrong in his methods:

"For the record," one female asserted, "I agree this is bullying. I do like that he went and got a free water though. I would have gone, gotten a free water, and had just said, 'I'm here to support Gay rights and protest against Chick-Fil-A's giving money to hate groups.' Period. And driven away. That's it. His statements are ridiculous and the poor girl!"

Perhaps no one reacted to it more negatively than his employer, Vante, a medical device manufacturing company that is located in Tuscon. Smith, who served as the company's CFO, was swiftly terminated the following day.

Vante released a statement assuring the public that Smith was "no longer an employee of our company." Among other things, the statement said that Vante "expect [s] our company officers to behave in a manner commensurate with their position and in a respectful fashion that conveys these values of civility with others."

After the sea of negative reaction to his first video, apparently Smith felt compelled to post a second. Yet this time, the Chick-Fil-A employee—who has only agreed to release her first name, Rachel—was the object, not of his hostilities, but of his remorse.

"Rachel," Smith begins, "I am so very sorry for the way I spoke to you on Wednesday. You handled my frustrating rant with such dignity and composure. Every time I watch the video I am blown away by really the beauty in what you did, and your kindness, and your patience with me."

Rachel was not ready to meet with Smith before.

Yet she is now.

Speaking to Smith's videoed apology, Rachel told FoxNews.com on August 7 that she is "definitely interested in" meeting with Smith.

"I appreciate that he came forward," she asserted. However, she now wants a chance to speak with Smith personally in order to "see if he was sincere [.]" Rachel also wants to "let him know why I handled" their unpleasant encounter "the way I did and not take legal action, which a lot of people told me I should do."

Rachel was as composed and kind during her interview with Fox as she was while being assailed by Smith. Even though she was unfairly bullied, she nevertheless refused to take legal action against Smith because she didn't think that there was any "reason to drag him through the mud any more than he has been."

It is hard not to be struck by the glaring contrast between Rachel and Smith. The decorum with which Rachel has conducted herself throughout this ordeal is the decorum that customers have come to expect from the employees of Chick-Fil-A.

And it is conduct that is in keeping with the restaurant's Christian character.

Rachel identifies her attitude succinctly: "I'm Christian and God tells us to love thy neighbor."

This being said, it is a mistake to suppose—as Smith supposed—that Chick-Fil-A imposes some sort of litmus test upon its employees. Rachel is quick to clarify this point:

"I'd really like to know if he [Smith] could separate the issue [of same sex marriage] from me and the company. The workers have nothing to do with the political beliefs with people in the corporation."

Furthermore, Rachel asserted that she most definitely does not "want to be part of that puzzle."

CHAPTER V

Christianity and Culture

Christian Politicians & Abortion

NEAR THE CLOSE of the Vice Presidential debate in Kentucky in 2012, moderator Martha Raddatz asked Vice President Joe Biden and Congressman Paul Ryan about the relationship between their faith and their politics.

What she really wanted to know about, though, is their respective views on abortion. Biden and Ryan are both self-avowed Roman Catholics. As such, one would expect that the Church's 2,000 year-old prohibition of abortion would count for something by their lights. And, to hear them both tell it, it does indeed. Biden *and* Ryan insisted that, along with Catholics past and present, they reject abortion. Biden's answer was particularly interesting.

"With regard to—with regard to abortion, I accept my church's position on abortion as a—what we call de fide. Life begins at conception. That's the church's judgment. I accept it in my personal life."

To judge just from these remarks, the Vice President's position on this issue appears unequivocal: he accepts the Catholic

Church's view that abortion is an intrinsically immoral act. However, not unlike every other prominent contemporary Catholic Democrat, Biden is quick to qualify his stance with the assurance that, unlike his opponent, he would never attempt to "impose" *his faith* upon others.

"But I refuse to impose it on equally devout Christians and Muslims and Jews and—I just refuse to impose that on others, unlike my friend here, the congressman." Furthermore, Biden adds, "I do not believe that—that we have a right to tell other people," particularly women, that "they—they can't control their body."

So, while Biden claims that he agrees with the Church's judgment that a human life comes into existence at conception, and agrees that abortion is an evil, he refuses to allow this to affect how he conducts himself in public life.

Biden's position is representative of that taken by virtually every contemporary Catholic Democrat. It is as intellectually inconsistent as it is morally abominable. The Catholic Church judges abortion as an evil simply and solely because it consists in the unjustified destruction of that innocent human life that began at conception. Abortion, that is, is evil for the same reason that it is immoral to unjustifiably destroy any human being—regardless of whether he is in the womb or outside of it.

In other words, if Biden is sincere about agreeing with the teaching of his Church on abortion, then he has just as much an obligation to do what he can to prevent the destruction of unborn human beings as he has an obligation to prevent the destruction of those human beings who have already been born. If it is somehow immoral for him to "impose" his view of abortion on others, then it is equally immoral for him to impose his view on murder and war as well.

Of course, it isn't just Democrats whose thought on abortion is an incoherent mess. Republicans don't fare much better on this score. Paul Ryan expressed the GOP's standard position when, during his debate with the Vice President, he said that he opposes abortion in all instances except for those of rape, incest, and when the pregnancy endangers the life of the mother. These exceptions, however, are hardly self-justifying. If abortion is immoral because it consists in the destruction of an innocent human being, then the circumstances in which that life came to be are both logically and morally irrelevant to its innocence. Indeed, there is nothing within either the Catholic teaching on abortion that the Ryans of the Republican Party claim to embrace or *the Republican Party's own platform* on this issue that would countenance abortion under virtually any circumstances. In 2012, the year that Ryan and Biden had their exchange, the GOP platform read: "Faithful to the 'self-evident' truths enshrined in the Declaration of Independence, we assert the sanctity of human life and affirm that the unborn child has a fundamental individual right to life that cannot be infringed."

As for Catholicism, Dr. Pia de Solenni sums up this point succinctly. Dr. de Solenni is an ethicist and cultural analyst who received her doctorate degree in sacred theology from the Pontifical University of the Holy Cross in Rome. In 2001, she received from Pope John Paul II the Award of the Pontifical Academies for her dissertation. On her blog, she writes of rape that it "has nothing to do with the human dignity of the fetus. Both the fetus and the mother deserve much better than rape, but neither of their lives is worth any less insofar as they are victims."

This reasoning holds as well for incest and the endangerment of the mother's life: The worth of a human being is not diminished because of circumstances over which he could not possibly have had any control. The unborn is innocent, and this innocence is not mitigated by the conditions in which conception and pregnancy occur.

Needless to say, not everyone agrees.

Jack Kerwick

The Definitive Case against Abortion

On Friday, January 27, 2017, masses of people converged on Washington D.C. to repudiate *Roe v Wade,* the 1973 Supreme Court decision that endowed upon American women a Constitutional "right" to "abortion."

With respect to most of the issues of the day, I can understand and appreciate, even if I do not accept, the reasons that my opponents give for the erroneous positions that they hold. The so-called issue of "abortion," however, is decidedly not one of them.

There are few topics that are framed from the outset in so many deceptive terms as is the topic of "abortion." Even its name, the label that both its proponents and *opponents* use when addressing this issue, is designed to veil the hideous reality that occurs when women exercise this "right" that a handful of lawyers on the Supreme Court created for them 44 years ago.

For the purpose of convenience, I too will defer to common usage and refer to the topic under discussion as "abortion." That being said, an honest discussion, to say nothing of decency, requires that we expose the euphemisms for what they are. "Abortion," "the right to choose," "a *woman's* right to choose," "a woman's right to choose to *'terminate the pregnancy'* or "abort *the fetus*"—these are the sorts of deceptive abstractions in which the advocates of abortion routinely trade.

In any other context, whether war, capital punishment, a school shooting, or whatever, when one party kills, or threatens to kill, another, we never say of the one party that it *aborted* or threatened to *abort* the other. Rival mobsters and gang-bangers don't seek to abort one another. President Trump didn't pledge to abort the Islamic State from the face of the Earth. American and Nazi soldiers weren't trying to abort each other. In all of these instances, it is understood that it is the activity of killing that is the essential referent.

Now, some acts of killing are morally defensible. The point, though, is that regardless of whether the killing in question is justifiable or not, no one thinks to describe it as an abortion unless and except for when it is a woman pursuing the death of her unborn child.

And this brings us to our next point: That abortion advocates must rely upon a host of impersonal terms to sustain their position is telling commentary. The truth, though, is that no woman "chooses" to exercise her "right" to "terminate *the* pregnancy" or "*the* fetus" (notice the unwillingness on the part of proponents to even characterize the unborn as *her* pregnancy or *her* fetus).

The cold, hard reality is that abortion consists in a *mother* hiring a stranger to kill, by whichever means necessary, *her child.*

Let this sink in. Those who support abortion maintain that it is morally permissible, perhaps even virtuous, that mothers resolve to have their children massacred. That the child is in the womb and at an earlier stage of development than it would otherwise eventually reach is, both ontologically and morally, of zero relevance. The tiny human being growing in its mother's womb differs from the reader of this essay similarly to the ways in which babies, toddlers, school children, and any other number of people differ from the reader of this essay. That is to say, prenatal human beings differ from post-natal human beings only *in degree.* Words like "fetus" disingenuously imply that the unborn child differs in kind from the rest of us.

In other words, it is meant, ludicrously, to suggest that, at the very least, the child in the womb is of a different *species.* Yet even this is probably understatement, for many of those who are the most vocal, indeed, fanatical of animal and environmental rights activists would recoil in horror if animals were subjected to the savagery—the hacking into pieces—that is visited upon the unborn in abortion procedures. Nor would they tolerate it if even plants were treated with the indifference with which the unborn are treated.

"Fetus" can have the hypnotic effect of luring people into thinking that the unborn do not belong to an organic species at all, that they are more on the order of masses of tissue, of things.

Abortion is most definitely *not* an issue of a "woman's choice over her own body." For that matter, neither is it, strictly speaking, an issue about some abstraction called "life." Rather, the question of abortion is nothing less than the question of whether we are going to affirm a world that encourages mothers to love and care for their children or one within which they feel entitled to kill them.

To reiterate, the relevant relationship here is not that of one rights-bearing individual to that of another. And it is certainly not the relationship between a human person and a non-person. Rather, the relationship on which the abortion issue hinges is that between a mother and her child.

Still, the mother/child relationship does not exist in a vacuum. A society that permits abortion speaks volumes about itself. In embracing the incoherent metaphysics of the childless pregnant woman (a pregnant woman with a "fetus," a mother without any obligations to the child that grows within her womb); in recognizing in women a "right" to kill their unborn children, society as a whole determines how it as well views the relationship between the strong and the weakest of the weak, the powerful and the most powerless of the powerless, the present generation and the next.

To be sure, far from being a moral right, abortion is undoubtedly the gravest of evils, for it expresses society's decision to treat its posterity, while at their most vulnerable, as disposable.

Christianity and the West

A group that refers to itself as the "Arkansas Society of Freethinkers" is not in the Christmas spirit. When it caught wind of the fact that Little Rock's Terry Elementary School had arranged for its students to attend a stage performance of "A Charlie Brown Christmas" at a local church, it began to eye the school up for a lawsuit.

Inasmuch as one of its key characters quotes the Gospel of Luke, "A Charlie Brown Christmas," you see, has an explicitly religious theme.

That there is no such "separation" clause in the United States Constitution has long been established. Yet this episode is telling not because it reveals the atheist's ignorance of the Constitution. Rather, it is telling insofar as it reveals his ignorance of his cultural inheritance.

The great Catholic writer, Hilaire Belloc, had famously declared that "the faith is Europe and Europe is the faith." We can paraphrase him by saying just as assuredly that Christianity is the West and the West is Christianity.

It is true that the Western mind is indebted to classical, pre-Christian Greek and Roman sources, but even here, it is primarily to Christian men of learning to whom we owe thanks for resurrecting and restoring to European civilization the lost riches of antiquity.

For the last two millennia there has been no aspect of Western existence that hasn't borne upon it the indelible impress of the Christian religion.

Take science. That it is the Western world within which the sciences first emerged and where they continue to flourish is no coincidence. Prior to the rise of Judaism (from which Christianity spun off), and outside of the Christian West to this day, time is conceived cyclically, not linearly. But it is our linear conception of time that inspires the scientist's faith in the possibility of achieving progress within his craft.

There are still other distinctively Christian concepts from which science has taken flight.

That the universe has been created by an all-good God and that this God has entrusted its care to the custody of human beings render it impossible for those who've been influenced by these beliefs to deny the reality of the world, as do Hindus and Buddhists, or to assume an attitude of indifference toward it, as did the Stoics. These Christian beliefs make it impossible to proclaim, with Plato and his disciples, that matter is somehow debased and, thus, unworthy of investigation. They make it impossible to deny the rationality of the world and, hence, the knowledge to be gotten from it.

The very (scientific) enterprise at which the scientist makes his living would have been unthinkable in the absence of the religious faith that he now ignores, and—far too frequently—disdains. Furthermore, he continues to erect his monuments upon the back of the Christian faith, for the supposition that nature is knowable and worth studying makes sense only within a larger Christian context. Once it has been plucked from that framework, however, then it is about as meaningful as a piece of a puzzle without the puzzle to which it belongs.

And what is true of the ideas underlying science are no less true of those of our morality.

The famed Russian novelist Dostoyevsky had said that if there is no God, then all things are possible. Dostoyevsky was a Christian. Yet some honest atheists—like the existentialist philosopher, Jean Paul Sartre—have admitted that he was correct.

"Indeed," Sartre wrote, it is precisely because "everything is permissible if God does not exist" that existentialist atheists like himself find life "very distressing [.]" Since there is no God, "all possibility of finding values in a heaven of ideas disappears along with Him [.]" There are "no values or commands" that "legitimize our conduct," there is "no excuse behind us, nor justification before us," for "we are alone...."

If Christianity is to go the way of the dinosaur, so too must natural law, natural rights, human rights, the Good, the True, and the Beautiful, and each and every one of our traditional moral ideals go this route, for without the theological *gestalt* supplied by Christianity, these ideals are reduced to arbitrary human inventions.

This Christmas season, let the "free thinkers" among us recognize that nothing that we take for granted—including our thought—is free. The price we pay for the goods we value is civilization, and for this civilization of ours we owe an eternal debt of gratitude to the very religion that too many of our "free thinkers" are intent upon destroying.

Atheism, Theism, and Morality

Where was God when Adam Lanza went on a shooting spree at an elementary school in Newtown, Connecticut that left 20 children and six adults dead?

Atheists assume that if there is evil in the world, then there can be no God. What they need to realize, however, is that if there is no God, then there can be no morality. This is what Dostoyevsky meant when he noted that if there is no God, then anything is possible.

Morality is *objective.* It consists of *norms* that are held to be *independent* of human will. Morality is not about what we do, or what we want to do. It is about what we *ought* to do—whether we want to do it or not.

But if there is no God, the Supreme Law Giver and Goodness Itself, then morality loses the only objective ground available to it—and, hence, itself.

Not so, many have retorted. Morality is rooted in *reason,* or *human nature,* or *biology.*

None of this will do. Reason, human nature, and biology may very well have a role to play in the moral life, but only if they are somehow ordained by God.

Reason is fickle. Over the centuries, distinguished thinkers—from Burke and De Maistre to Hobbes and Hume to Montaigne and Pascal—representing a variety of philosophical traditions have recognized this. Adolph Hitler and Osama bin Laden (and Adam Lanza, for that matter) acted no less rationally in the pursuit of their goals than did Mother Teresa and Gandhi act in the pursuit of theirs. Reason is all too easily, and frequently, subverted by the simplest of things, whether passion, impulse, fear, or sickness.

Those who would attempt to use reason as the foundation upon which to lay morality are like a man who tries to build a house on quicksand.

And what is true of reason is just as true of human nature and biology.

Human nature has its angels, for sure, but it also has its demons. Any human being who has dared to look honestly at himself will be compelled to acknowledge this stone cold fact. As we *all* say: No one is perfect.

Biology is even less eligible of a candidate for a basis of morality. Biology gives us instincts and impulses, needs and inclinations—in short, *causes* of various sorts. Yet it cannot supply *reasons.*

Biology *compels.* Morality, in stark contrast, presupposes the *freedom* to make *choices.*

If there is no God, then there is no spirit. And if there is no spirit, then all is matter: reason and human nature boil down to human biology, and biology, in turn, becomes nothing more or less than the latest product of a resolutely non-purposeful mechanical process billions of years in the happening.

Christianity and the World

If there is no God, then anything is possible.

It isn't just Dostoyevsky, a Christian, who recognized this. Some of the most astute and staunchest of atheists have as well.

Of Christianity, Friedrich Nietzsche said that he regarded it "as the most fatal and seductive lie that has ever yet existed—as the greatest and most *impious lie*." Yet Nietzsche viewed Christianity as the ground zero of the "campaign against morality" that he openly waged, the prototype of just the notion of objective morality that he so despised.

Thus, when Nietzsche declared "the death of God," it was the death of moral objectivity, of moral absolutes, that he celebrated.

Human beings had nothing to go on but their own "Will to Power." They alone are *the creators* of value.

Jean Paul Sartre was even clearer on this score.

Though an atheist, he scoffed at those atheists who held that we could preserve such traditional moral ideals as honesty, compassion, and justice while doing away with belief in God. Rather, he admitted to finding it "very distressing that God does not exist, because all possibility of finding values in a heaven of ideas disappears along with him [.]" If there is no God, then there are "no values or commands," no principles or ideals, that "legitimize our conduct."

Sartre's verdict is as haunting as it is inescapable. If there is no God, then we "are alone, with no excuses."

The response of believer and unbeliever alike to Adam Lanza's shooting spree in Connecticut is unmistakably *moral* in character. Yet unless God exists, there is no basis for our conviction that it was an act of evil.

And unless the atheist, in his own peculiar way, needed God as much as anyone else, he wouldn't feel compelled to look beyond his world of material causes and cosmic insignificance to blame Him for not existing.

"Jesus Now"

Easter Sunday is fast approaching.

While Christmas and Easter are inseparable from one another, and while the latter could not have occurred without the former having first occurred, there is no question that for the Christian world there is no event of greater significance than that of Easter.

Christmas is the celebration of the Incarnation, God's assumption of human flesh in the Person of Jesus of Nazareth. Easter, however, is the celebration of the main point to which Christmas points, God's glorious Resurrection from the dead.

Easter assures us that death has been defeated and that all who believe in Christ have been graced with, not just immortality, but eternity, timelessness union, with God.

There is no greater news. There is no greater reward than any human creature could ever hope to attain.

This being said, although the eternal life that God the Father offers the human race through the sacrifice of God the Son is a *gift*, and even though God Himself paid a price for it that human beings could never afford to pay, there *is* a cost, a great cost, that people must expend if they wish to avail themselves of God's infinite bounty.

That cost is nothing more or less than their whole selves, their minds, hearts, and souls.

Of course, there is also a cost to *not* believing in Christ. If you didn't read the Gospels carefully, if you just relied on the homilies or sermons of far too many contemporary clerics, whether Catholic or Protestant, you wouldn't know this, but the cost of rejecting Christ is nothing other than *the loss* of eternal life.

Again, this is hardly a popular message. Christian clergy know all too well that in the Western world of the 21st century, to stress from their pulpits the violent streak in Jesus's teachings, His continual, frightening evocations of the eternal condemnation to which unbelievers will be subject, is to risk losing no small share of their congregations. Doubtless, a good number of these ministers don't want to reckon themselves with this aspect of their Savior's message.

But reckon it with we must, for to deny this feature of Christ is to substitute for the Christ of the Gospels something inevitably less than the real thing, an idol made in the image of our own contemporary sensibilities. The Jesus with whom millions of American Christians are familiar is a sentimentalized, one-dimensional caricature that, by design, is as non-threatening as he is boring.

This Jesus—let's call him "Jesus Now"—is decidedly incongruent to both the Jesus that unfolds in the pages of the New Testament as well as the Jesus recognized by the Church of yesteryear. The differences are numerous.

Jesus Now spent his ministry on Earth traveling the countryside doing nothing but preaching…*love*. It's true that the real Jesus did so as well. Only "love" is interpreted very differently depending on whether it is Jesus Now or the real Jesus who is preaching it.

The love with which Jesus Now is preoccupied isn't something that either the real Jesus or any other human being that has ever lived would recognize. There are certainly some people who have spoken *as if* they knew what it is. For example, those secular, leftist "progressives" who are the ideological offspring of 1960's hippies can certainly identify with Jesus Now, for, theoretically speaking (their actual practice is all too typically an entirely different matter), they embrace the same vapid, nonjudgmental, and indiscriminate fluffy stuff associated with the "love" of Jesus Now.

This is an utterly thoughtless "love," a "love" that, being without expectations, obligations, distinctions, and consequences, would have to exist in total abstraction from real relationships. St.

John the Evangelist said in his gospel that God is love. From the perspective of Jesus Now and his present-day disciples, "Love" is God.

In stark contrast, the real Jesus *and every other human being* who has ever known real (if imperfect) love knows that love is, well, *tough*. Consider the parent-child relationship. Intimations of God's love for those who He made in His image are ubiquitous throughout His creation. Yet it wasn't until I became a father to my son that I genuinely felt something that I imagine is analogous to God's love for us. There are moments, usually when he is sleeping at night, when I still feel overwhelmed to the point of tears with my love for my boy.

Yet it is precisely because of this love that I discipline my son when he misbehaves. It is from my unconditional love for him—and it truly is unconditional—that my expectations for my son arise. To most parents the truth of what I say is obvious: Far from being incompatible with love, the latter demands that we correct, castigate, and, when necessary, punish our children. Parents who dare to practice Jesus Now's version of "love," who refuse to pass judgment, refuse to discipline, and/or who refuse to discriminate between their own children and the children of total strangers, are not fit to be parents.

As every person who has ever been married can readily attest, spousal love, though a fundamentally different species of love than that at the heart of the parent-child relationship, is even further removed from the "love" of Jesus Now. Spousal love consists of mutual obligations, rights, and responsibilities. Spouses hold each other to account for their actions. There *are* consequences to violating one's duties to one's spouse.

We could continue.

It's not just that the "love" of Jesus Now is unrealistic. It is positively boring. If it is correct that Jesus did nothing but preach "love," then, the remotely curious person must ask, why in the world would anyone pay attention to Him, to say nothing of go out of their way to kill Him?

Another difference between Jesus Now and real Jesus is that the gospel of the former is virtually indistinguishable from the Political Correctness that is the reigning orthodoxy of contemporary Western elites. To hear our clerics tell it, one could be forgiven for thinking that Jesus endorses government mandated preferential treatment policies for racial minorities, women, and homosexuals; the erasure of all national boundaries; and limitless illegal immigration.

Jesus Now is a full-throated pacifist. He opposes the death penalty and war.

In the days leading up to Easter, I pray that more Christians see Jesus Now for the PC fiction that he is and make it a point to come to know, perhaps for the very first time, the Jesus that is their Savior.

The Real Jesus

In a recent article, I delineated the features of a figure to which I referred as "Jesus Now."

Jesus Now is the Jesus, perhaps the only Jesus, with whom millions of contemporary American Christians are familiar. Churchgoers are no different in this respect, for it is from their clerics that they hear about Jesus Now week after week.

Jesus Now is a man of our times, a liberal progressive whose Politically Correct moral and political sensibilities are unassailable. He preaches "tolerance," "inclusivity," and, importantly, he is "non-judgmental." Moreover, Jesus Now is largely indifferent to whether people even believe in him—just so long as they are "good" people.

Of course, it is not quite correct to say of Jesus Now that he judges no one. But his judgment is extremely selective. He adversely judges white, affluent, Western Christians. Everyone else is given a pass.

In glaring contrast, the Real Jesus (who will be referred to from now on simply as "Jesus"), being the Author of the Heavens and the Earth, the Sovereign Ruler of all creation, is the Judge Incarnate.

Jesus is hardly the meek and mild, the non-threatening (and wildly boring) fiction that is peddled in all too many churches. Actually, He spends quite a bit of time—most, it seems—expressing *anger*. On at least one occasion, such was Jesus's indignation that He engaged in conduct that would land me or you in jail:

When merchants were doing what they always did and engaged in commercial activities in the Temple, Jesus besieged them, knocking over their tables and displays and driving them out with a whip.

Jesus was as scathing toward His disciples as He was toward His opponents. He continually castigated His friends and followers alike for their lack of faith and, during His Sermon on the Mount, referred to them as "evil" (Lk 11:13). Peter, on whom He would build His church, He called "Satan" when the former implored his master to avoid His impending death (Mt 16:23). This generation, Jesus remarked, was both "evil and adulterous" (Mt 16:4).

He called His rivals, the scribes and Pharisees, "hypocrites," "blind guides," "blind fools," "whitewashed tombs," "snakes," and a "brood of vipers." "How," the Real Jesus asked them, "can you escape being sentenced to hell?" (Mt 23: 1-36; Mk 12:38-40; Lk 20-45-47).

Nor was this the only time, or the scribes and Pharisees His only rivals, with whom Jesus threatened *eternal* violence.

During the Great Commission, He instructed His disciples to turn their backs on those who refused to welcome them, "to shake off the dust from your feet as you leave that house or town." Jesus assured them: "Truly I tell you, it will be more tolerable for the land of Sodom and Gomorrah [cities that God destroyed] on the day of the judgment than for that town" (Mt 10:1-15; Mk 3:13-19; Lk 6:12-16).

As for the residents of those cities in which Jesus performed "deeds of power" but who refused to repent, He promises to visit destruction upon them. "Woe to you, Chorazin! Woe to you, Bethsaida! For if the deeds of power done in you had been done in Tyre and Sidon [more cities that had been destroyed by God], they would have repented long ago...." But because there has been no repentance, the fate of these cities will be *worse* than that of the cities of yesteryear that God eliminated.

Capernaum, the city in which Jesus spent no small share of His time, is going to have it just as badly. "And you, Capernaum, will you be exalted to Heaven? No, you will be brought down to Hades" (Mt 11: 20-24; Lk 10:13-15).

Jesus frequently spoke in parables invoking the imagery of slavery and war.

To allude to just one parable, Jesus contrasts the faithful and wise slave with the unfaithful and wicked one. The former is dutiful and prepares for his master's return home. The latter is lazy and nasty to his fellow slaves. Of the wicked slave, Jesus tells us, his "master...will cut him in pieces and put him with the hypocrites, where there will be weeping and gnashing of teeth" (Mt 24:45-51; Lk 12:41-48).

Regarding the cost of discipleship, Jesus said: "Or what king, going out to wage war against another king, will not sit down first and consider whether he is able with ten thousand to oppose the one who comes against him with twenty thousand?" (Lk 14: 31).

He encouraged—commanded, in fact—His disciples to arm themselves with swords (Lk 22:36).

As for ecumenism, the Real Jesus was having none of it: There would be no half-measures when it came to belief in Him. Either one believed in Him or one did not. He promised to bring, not peace, but "the sword." He promised that He would divide human beings in a manner and to a degree that had never been seen.

"For I have come to set a man against his father, and a daughter against her mother, and a daughter-in-law against her mother-in-law; and one's foes will be members of one's own household."

Jesus is unequivocal: If anyone loves any of their family members more than they love Him, they are unworthy of Him. For such folks, there will be no eternal life (Mt 10: 34-39; Lk 12:51-53; 14: 26-27).

Even those who are convinced of their own Christian discipleship and who perform good works may find themselves being denied eternity with God. "Not everyone who says to me, 'Lord, Lord,' will enter the kingdom of heaven, but only the one who does the will of my Father in heaven," He tells us. "On that day [the Day of Judgment] many will say to me, 'Lord, Lord, did we not prophesy in your name, and cast out demons in your name, and do many deeds of power in your name?'" Jesus gives us His answer: "Then I will declare to them, 'I never knew you; go away from me, you evildoers'" (Mt. 7:21-23; Lk 13: 26-27).

Between the Real Jesus and Jesus Now, it should be obvious, there is an unbridgeable chasm.

The Young Messiah

The Young Messiah (*TYM*) is a film at once entertaining and endearing. An admittedly fictionalized imagining of Jesus as a seven year-old boy, this movie's treatment of its subject matter is eminently respectful.

Not everyone feels this way, however.

Dave Armstrong, a "professional Catholic apologist," concedes in *Patheos* that "there are several aspects of [the] *development* of the human knowledge of Jesus...that are legitimate

Christianity and the World

and perfectly orthodox [.]" It is, though, *un*orthodox and, hence, *il*legitimate to depict Christ as "*growing into...* awareness" of His identity, for the Church has affirmed for centuries that, from conception, Jesus *knew that He was God* (italics added).

Armstrong quotes Neil Madden who, writing at *Conservative Review,* makes the following remark:

"'The Young Messiah'" depicts Mary and Joseph as having more knowledge about Jesus's true nature than He does. This is a problem. If Jesus was always God, begotten and not made, surely wouldn't an omnipotent God know who he was as he was learning and growing in preparation for His mission here on Earth?"

Though Armstrong doesn't seem to notice it, he and Madden are actually making two distinct points. Armstrong's point is that Jesus, *in His humanity*, knew that He was God from the time that He was conceived. Madden, on the other hand, refers to Jesus *in His divinity*.

Doubtless, this controversy stems from nothing less than the *mystery* of the uniquely Christian doctrine of the Incarnation, the doctrine that God became a human being in Jesus: Christ is "true God and true man," fully divine and fully human.

Two replies to *TYM's* critics are in the coming.

First, if Neil Madden is correct that Jesus, being "an omnipotent God" must have always known His own identity "as he was learning and growing in preparation for His mission here on Earth," then there would've been no "*learning* and *growing* in preparation" for that mission, for "an omnipotent God" would've had *already* known *all* that could be known about *everything* and *anything.*

On the other hand, if the "omnipotence" of Christ *in His divinity* is compatible with Christ *in His humanity* coming to learn and grow in *some* matters, then it is, in principle, compatible with Christ as *fully human* coming to learn and grow in *all* matters.

Secondly, unlike Madden, Armstrong alludes to Christ in His humanity, Christ *at conception.* Yet even here it is a mistake to

117

think that if Christ knew from conception that He was God that He could *not* have grown into an awareness of His identity.

The two propositions do not necessarily contradict one another—as long as "knowledge" isn't construed in an unduly shallow sense.

From at least the time of Plato throughout the centuries until Freud and beyond, a great many thinkers (and non-thinkers alike) have been of the mind that knowledge can be explicit and implicit, conscious and *un*conscious. Examples abound to suggest that this position has something going for it.

Take, for instance, what is known as "the principle of non-contradiction," the principle that a thing can't be and not be in the same respect and at the same time, that "(A) and (non-A)" *must* be false. Though most people outside of philosophy and logic classes have never heard of this principle, everyone knows it, for it is the most fundamental law of all thought.

Students must "grow into an awareness" of the principle of non-contradiction. And yet they've *known* it all of their lives.

If knowing could consist in human subjects growing into an awareness of (at least some of) what they already implicitly know, then how much more fitting would such an approach be regarding the God-Man? Consider: As God, Christ would had to have known all things from eternity. As a man, Christ would have to have grown and developed like all humans—even if that knowledge was already in Him from conception.

In conclusion, *TYM's* portrayal of Jesus as learning His divine identity from Joseph and Mary is compatible with the position that, *in His divinity,* He always knew His identity. It's also compatible with the idea that Christ, *in His humanity*, knew His identity from conception.

The only position that the thesis of *TYM* obviously contradicts is the thesis that Jesus, *in His humanity,* or from *conception,* was *fully conscious* of his divine nature, for if this thesis was true, then it would've indeed been logically impossible for Jesus to have *grown into* a consciousness of His identity.

The Young Messiah doesn't deviate at all from theological orthodoxy when it comes to the question of Jesus's knowledge of His own divine identity.

Christian Duties

Catholic Churches in the greater Philadelphia area where I live are eagerly preparing for Pope Francis' visit to Philly.

While at Mass this Sunday, the officiating priest—who also happens to be a professor of "Christian anthropology" at a local Catholic university and a die-hard Pope Francis fan—gave a homily that provided me with some food for thought.

Christians, he said, are called upon to care for "the poor" and the most "marginalized" by "society." We are called upon to care for those who can't care properly for themselves.

On its face, this will doubtless strike many as nothing more or less than standard Christian teaching. Equally doubtless is that this is the stuff of which the contemporary homily or sermon consists.

But this is the problem.

Of course, Christians do indeed have a duty in Christ and to Christ to serve "the poor." But this is only because Christians have a duty in Christ and to Christ to serve anyone and everyone who is in need.

This is a crucial point to grasp.

To hear my priest (and countless others just like him) tell it—and repeatedly tell it—unless a person can be lumped into one of the categories that he specifies, unless a person is among "the marginalized," the disciples of Christ haven't any obligation at all to that person, or at least no obligation to attend to the person's needs.

In other words, as a Christian, do I not have a duty to care for the powerful, the wealthy, and the healthy, for those who are recognized, respected, and even celebrated by society? Christian clerics like my priest from this Sunday would have me think not.

This is not a matter of being sophistic or otherwise deliberately obtuse, for Christian clerics—whether Catholic priests or Protestant ministers (but especially the former)—*never, ever* talk about loving the rich and mighty. *Never.* To the contrary, the latter are spoken of critically, sometimes to the point of demonization.

Certainly it's the case that clerics remind disciples of the duty to "visit the imprisoned," but either implicitly or explicitly, the imprisoned are linked to "the poor." In impressing this connection upon their congregants, ministers seek to insure that the often brutal, horrific circumstances that lead to the long-term imprisonment of most prisoners escape the minds of their flocks.

Also, by identifying prisoners with "the poor," Christian leaders inculcate feelings of sympathy, and possibly even of *guilt*, by suggesting that convicted criminals are actually *victims* of a cruel, un-Christian society that has "marginalized" them.

The implication of this message that contemporary Christian ministers routinely drill into the brains of their congregants is that poor murderers and rapists are more deserving of compassion and empathy than are rich CEO's.

The Bible, neither the Old nor the New Testaments, supplies no support for this lopsided vision that prevails in so much of contemporary American Christianity. *King* David, for example, was both super wealthy and powerful, and yet he is a great Biblical hero, a man after God's heart. King Solomon was the richest of men—and also among the wisest. Solomon is no less great in stature than was his father.

When God went in search of a House in which to dwell on Earth—i.e. the Temple—it is to the super wealthy and powerful that He turned.

Christianity and the World

These are just two of the more notable illustrations of the profoundly wealthy and powerful among God's blessed.

In the New Testament, Jesus attends to the needs of the rich and powerful as well as to those of the poor. The Roman soldier whose servant Christ saves is an agent—and a symbol—of the most powerful empire the world had ever known until that juncture. He also had to have been a man of considerable means if he was able to afford a servant.

Jesus also satisfied the needs of some of the movers and shakers of His day, specifically members of the Sanhedrin. The latter was the council of religious leaders that arranged to have Him executed by Rome, but Nicodemus and Joseph of Arimathea were among its member that became Christ's disciples. They pleaded for Christ's life and when such pleadings failed, it was Joseph who secured the tomb in which Jesus's body was laid.

Christ commissioned His apostles to make disciples of *all* nations, not just poor nations, and not just poor people. His apostles listened and endeavored to spread the Gospel to *all,* rich and poor, powerful and powerless, Jew and Gentile. The tacit and sometimes not so tacit class warfare that today's pulpit warriors seem fond of waging on Sunday mornings is one form of war with respect to which Jesus and His Apostles were pacifists.

There is another problem with this exclusive focus on "the poor" and "marginalized."

It is all too easy for Christians to neglect caring for their next door neighbors, relatives, and friends—with those with whom they are closest but whom are not materially "poor" or societally "marginalized." As long as they deploy some of their resources in time, energy, and money (but mostly money) to those beneath some bureaucratically-constructed poverty line, or some abstract category singled out by their ministers, it promises to be all too easy for them to rest assured that they've fulfilled their duties to Christ without further ado.

I suggest that, if we really want to encourage Christian charity, we drop (the excessively materialistic) references to serving "the poor" in favor of those to "the needy." Everyone is needy is some respects.

Christians are called upon to attend to the "needs" of all—not just "the poor."

Christianity, Hatred, and the Need to Judge

There is hardly a week that passes when Christian pastors and ministers from across denominations don't use their time at the pulpit to admonish their flocks to love as Christ loved. As the Christian world prepares itself for the Passion and Resurrection of its Savior during this Holy Week, such calls to love intensify.

To be certain, Christians are called—are commanded—by their Lord to *love*. As St. Paul said, of the three "theological" virtues, faith, hope, and love, the greatest of these is love.

But those of us who aspire to be the disciples of Jesus are also called to *hate*. In fact, it is precisely *because* we are called to love that we are called to hate, and to hate with every ounce of the zeal, the devotion, the aching, with which we are expected to love. The paradox here is only apparent:

The love of God and neighbor with which Christians are consumed is inseparable from the intense hatred of evil and sin demanded of them.

Yet Christians hear relatively little about their obligation in Christ to burn with hatred for corruption.

This is nothing short of a scandal.

First, while it is true that, as St. John said in his First Epistle, God *is* Love, it is equally true that God is Justice. The God of the Bible—both the *Old* Testament as well as the *New*—is a God of infinite compassion. But He is also a God who rewards and punishes. In stressing God's mercy at the expense of neglecting His wrath, Christians do a gross disservice to both, for divine mercy and divine wrath are meaningful only when each is understood in light of the other.

One can't know God unless one knows about His love *and* His justice.

Second, when justice *is* mentioned in connection with love in many Christian churches nowadays—particularly Roman Catholic churches like the one that I attend—it always refers to something that Christians from times past wouldn't have recognized as justice at all: so-called "*social* justice."

Yet social justice is what I will call *No* Justice. No Justice is a doctrine, favored by secular, atheistic leftists and far too many Christians alike, that the government must confiscate the resources in time, labor, and property from those to whom they belong and "redistribute" them to those who have less. This is the ugly reality of No Justice.

No Justice is injustice. Far from supporting "social justice," as a Christian, I am duty-bound to detest it. And I detest it for the same reason that I detest slavery: it is manifestly unjust for one person or group to coerce others, for whatever reasons, to part with the fruits of their labor.

It is unjust for one person or group to coerce others to subsidize activities to which the latter never consented and to which their consciences may very well be opposed.

But it is exactly this of which No Justice consists.

We should not be misled by any of this into thinking that it is only the evil of the government for which Christians are to reserve their hatred, much less that only government is capable of evil. The disciples of Jesus know as well as anyone that such is the ubiquity of evil in the world that it even infects their own hearts.

Still, while Christian clergy will talk much about sin in the abstract, they seem to studiously avoid mentioning many specifics. And even when they urge the members of their flocks to look within, they routinely counsel them to be "less judgmental" of others, and more mindful of their own sins. But turning a blind eye to the wickedness of others is a recipe for the perfection, *not* of virtue, but of vice.

It has not infrequently been noted—but not noted enough—that the vicious are a better source of moral guidance than are the virtuous. By way of his life sentence behind bars, a convict stands a far better chance of deterring a reckless adolescent male from a life of crime than that of his honest father who constantly pleads with his beloved son to walk the straight and narrow path. All of the Surgeon General's warnings regarding the potential dangers of cigarette smoking aren't going to persuade young, healthy smokers from indulging their habit of choice. The sight of a lifelong smoker suffering from lung cancer, however, might do the trick.

Similarly, for Christians to learn about and hate evil as they should, they *must* judge, and judge unequivocally, judge passionately, the wickedness of others. We first spot evil when it is outside of us, and it is vastly easier at that point to recognize it in all of its hideousness. Noticing and judging the evil of others is an indispensable step to noticing and judging the evil in our own hearts.

Noticing and judging the evil of others is an indispensable step to knowing and loving God and neighbor.

The Christian Roots of Contemporary Morality

Philadelphia Eagles' star Riley Cooper is the latest celebrity to have to issue an emotional, and very public, mea culpa for having used that most infamous of racial slurs, "the N-word." Fortunately for him, it appears that Cooper has been forgiven.

Christianity and the World

From these public apologies much can be learned—and a thing or two about contemporary American racial politics isn't even the most of it.

First, from the highest to the lowest, every aspect of our culture remains saturated in a distinctly *Christian* vision of morality.

The notion that it is gravely immoral to regard people differently, much less treat them badly, on the bases of race, ethnicity, gender, class, and even religion is a part of Christianity's legacy to the world. And it is the ubiquity of the belief in this idea that accounts for the pressure brought upon Cooper and others to repent of their transgressions.

In other words, if not for the world that Christianity produced, it is not likely that "racism," "sexism," "ethnocentrism," "classism," "ageism," "ableism," "classism," or any of the other "isms" that are deemed unmitigated evils by our public culture would have ever been conceived, to say nothing of actually observed.

Note, I do not mean to sugest that there's anything like a straight line that runs from an educated understanding of Christianity to the Politically Correct excesses of our day. And *I know* that, consciously speaking, the most zealous of "anti-racists" and their ilk are motivated by an *animus* toward Christianity—not a devotion to it.

No matter. The point is that while our PC zeitgeist is doubtless a *perversion* of Christianity, it is still a perversion *of Christianity*. If the aforementioned "isms" are unconscionable, it can only be because the differences on which they are based are *superficial*. That is, it must be the case that underlying our differences is a common human nature, a fundamental essence from which each and every person derives an inalienable dignity.

It is this belief, and only this belief, that informs not just belief in the awfulness of "racism" and the like. It is also only this belief that informs the widespread view that there is a "moral law" and "moral rights" of which *all* members of the human race are in possession.

But here's the rub: if there is such a thing as human dignity, then human beings are not, and can never be, the bio-chemical accidents of a purposeless, endless evolutionary process. This isn't to deny evolution, in some sense of this word. It *is* to deny the logical tenability of a theory according to which something called "human dignity" can emerge from a universe comprised of *nothing* but matter in motion.

In fact, as such staunch atheists as Friedrich Nietzsche and Jean Paul Sartre have remarked, the very notion of human nature itself is the offspring of Christianity. The concept of human nature serves the same function as the concept of God: both constrain individuals by specifying in advance limits on what they can do and who they can be. This similarity is no coincidence, for unless there is a God, an author of human nature, the latter can't exist.

But, as Sartre wrote, if there is no God, then "everything is permissible [.]" The great existentialist philosopher admitted that he found this view of reality "very distressing," for he recognized that it entailed that there are "no values or commands" that "legitimize our conduct [.]" It means that "we are alone [.]"

Nietzsche disdainfully referred to Christianity as the penultimate "slave morality" from which other species of slave morality like "Democracy," "socialism," and "liberalism" spun off. From the perspective of "the slave morality," the evil man is "the aristocrat, the powerful one, the one who rules [.]"

The slave-morality, on the other hand, affirms just those qualities that promise to alleviate its proponents' suffering: "sympathy, the kind, helping hand, the warm heart, patience, diligence, humility, and friendliness [.]" Because these are the characteristics that supply "the only means of supporting the burden of existence," they are elevated to the stature of universal human excellences.

If there is such a thing as human dignity, it can only be because humans were, as Christians say, made in the image of God.

The verdict is clear: whether we choose to recognize it or not, the fact of the matter is that upon our shared morality is the indelible impress of Christianity.

The latter's nemeses from yesteryear readily conceded this.

Apparently, their progeny today lack either their ancestors' honesty or their courage.

Christianity and Christmas

Christmas, unlike any other Western holiday, is ubiquitous. It is as impossible for an inhabitant of the Western world to escape Christmas as it is impossible for a person to escape breathing while remaining alive.

For this reason, Christmas is a microscopic expression of Christianity's relationship to the civilization to which it gave rise.

Both religious and irreligious alike celebrate Christmas. Few and far between are the residences, businesses, and even government buildings that aren't adorned with at least some decorative reminders of the season. Christmas music can be heard emanating from every conceivable medium while many television networks and movie theaters are taken over by Christmas-themed programs and films.

While it is true that many of the most widely recognized holiday symbols—talking snowmen, flying reindeer, Christmas trees, candy canes, elves, and even Santa Claus—are "secularized," the religious roots of the holiday are, or at least should be, unmistakable.

For starters, just the word "holiday" itself stems from *holy day,* a day that is supposed to be set aside for prayerful reflection. That, in the Western world, no holiday is as big of a deal as that of

Christmas serves as a reminder, however subtle, of the significance of the *holiness* of the occasion.

Secondly, "Christmas" means *the Mass* of *Christ*. With every mention of the word, then, the name of Christ—the "reason for the season"—is invoked.

Thirdly, the very notion, expressed *wherever* there's an expression of Christmas, that Christmas is a cause for celebration, a time for *miracles,* and a time to rejoice in song and gift-giving, derives from no other source other than the traditional Christian belief that God gave us the greatest gift of Himself through the miracle of the Incarnation. Christmas lights, the stars that we place at the tops of our trees, and even candy canes remind us of this: lights signify *the* Light of Christ; the Christmas tree star beckons back to the star that guided the Magi as they searched for the birth place of baby Jesus; and candy canes are designed to resemble the staff of Jesus, the Good Shepherd, its hardness signifying Jesus, the Rock, and its colors, red and white, pointing, respectively, toward the blood and purity of Christ.

Finally, we mustn't forget that Santa Claus, the most popular and visible of all "secular" symbols of Christmas, is rooted in the historical person of *Saint Nicholas,* a fourth century Christian bishop who, inspired by the example of his Lord and Savior, lived a life of selflessness.

Just as the stuff of which Christmas is made hearken us back to its Christian roots, so too does the stuff of which contemporary *Western civilization* is made hearken us back to *its* Christian roots.

Below are just some of our taken-for-granted ideas and institutions that are unmistakably Christian in origin:

(1) Each and every human being, irrespective of circumstances, possesses an inviolable dignity by virtue of having been created in the image of God. This idea is the core of a moral vision that, unlike its predecessors, extended its liberties and duties to *all* human beings. The tribalism of old had been eclipsed.

Christianity and the World

(2) Because of (1), we have a duty to extend *charity* to all, including total *strangers,* and even enemies: Overwhelmingly, charity is a distinctively *Christian* virtue. This explains why, even at present, charity remains a predominantly Christian phenomenon.

Anthony Esolen, author of *The Politically Incorrect Guide to Western Civilization,* writes: "Hindus do not send holy men into foreign lands to feed the hungry and house the naked: they will not do so for the pariahs *in their own land*" (emphasis mine). He adds: "Buddhists, practicing benevolent detachment from the world, do not do so. Muslims, who conquer by force, and who reject natural law on the grounds that it 'fetters' Allah, are required to take care of their own, but they ignore everyone else."

(3) The world (universe) is not cyclical, as the ancient pagans held, but rational and orderly. It is also not a vale of tears, but, as God declared it, "good." Thus, nature *could be* explored and *should be* explored. From these Christian suppositions, science, with all of its wondrous, life-saving technologies, took flight.

(4) The separation of "Church" and "State" sprung from the Christian's rejection of State worship and, of course, Jesus' admonition to pay unto Caesar his due, while giving God what is owed to *Him*.

(5) Many of the West's most historic philosophers, painters, composers, authors, and scientists derived their inspiration, their presuppositions regarding the characters of ultimate reality, knowledge, religion, and morality from the Christian worldview that they inherited. In the absence of Christianity, it is as inconceivable that our culture would be so much as *remotely* recognizable to itself as it is inconceivable that we would still be celebrating Christmas.

So, this Christmas, let's not only remember that Jesus made possible the occasion for this holiday. Let's remember as well that He made possible the very civilization, the most awesome of civilizations, that we call our own.

Jack Kerwick

Christianity and "Inequality"

That Jesus commanded His disciples—of which I am one—to love "the poor" is beyond dispute. Equally beyond dispute, however, is that, regardless of what growing legions of left-leaning clerics would have us believe, Jesus *never*—never *ever*—addressed the issue of "inequality."

The head of my church and the most visible religious leader on the world stage today, Pope Francis, is as guilty a culprit as is anyone on this score. The Pope made headlines on more than a few occasions since his tenure began when His Holiness condemned "inequality" generally, and the traditional American economic system in particular, with a bluntness that would have made Barack Hussein Obama blush.

Ours is "an economy of exclusion and inequality," Pope Francis insisted. Our system of "inequality" both results from and encourages "laws of competition and the survival of the fittest, where the powerful feed upon the powerless." Thus, "masses of people find themselves excluded and marginalized: without work, without possibilities, without any means of escape."

Worse, the Pope informs us, our "capitalist" system with its "inequality" violates the divine injunction against "killing," for "such an economy *kills*" (emphasis added).

Pope Francis may be the most well-known Christian leader to conflate Jesus' teachings on the proper treatment of *the poor* with the issue of income and wealth "inequalities." But he speaks for countless lesser known representatives of Christianity.

Take Norma Cook Everist, a professor of church and ministry. In an article that she penned for *The Lutheran,* Everist insists that things haven't changed a lick since Martin Luther said that "the poor" are routinely "defrauded" by "the rich."

"Inequality," Everist remarks, divides the world into "makers" and "takers" while fostering the godless fiction that some people, and even "some children," are "worth more" than others, and that some, "the poor," are of "'of no worth'[.]"

The project of reducing the Gospel to an activist's manual on addressing "inequality" is fraught with difficulties.

First, as already noted, it is simply *dishonest:* there is no basis, Biblical or otherwise, for equating an obligation to care for the poor with an obligation to endorse political policies ostensibly aimed at reducing "inequalities" in income and wealth. Decent minded people of all faiths and no faith have long recognized the need to care for those in poverty, and Christians specifically have always been acutely aware of this as a moral imperative.

But it hasn't been until the emergence of large, centralized governments, immensely affluent, industrialized societies, and the dominance of secular, egalitarian ideologies—i.e. phenomena that don't appear until relatively late in Christian history—that anyone, much less any Christian cleric, has thought to identify compassion for the poor with the amelioration of "inequalities."

Second, even the tireless emphasis that pastors place upon Jesus' relationship with "the poor" is less than fully honest, for it is grounded in a selective reading of the New Testament.

"The poor" is as ambiguous as it is emotionally-charged a term. Most of the people among whom Jesus spent His time were certainly not rich by the standards of their day, and some of them did indeed live in grinding poverty. While it's true that there was no "middle class," it's equally true that just because the tax collectors, farmers, fishermen, carpenters and so forth with whom He appears to have fraternized were not rich, neither were they all impoverished.

That today's clerics fail to make these discriminations between those to whom Jesus ministered by referring to them all as "the poor" reflects their awareness of the emotional *and* moral appeal of this moniker. After all, "the poor" are, well, poor: only the heartless could fail to feel for them. And "the poor" also lends those so designated moral authority, for being the *victims* of their circumstances, "the poor" are always *blameless*.

Third, this *exclusive stress* on Jesus' fondness for "the poor," whether by accident or design, conveys the impression that He was *exclusively fond* of "the poor," a respecter of persons by virtue of their socio-economic condition—exactly what the Bible insists God *is not*.

This notion, in turn, further underscores a sense of moral superiority among "the poor" by fueling it with the fiction that their poverty is a saving grace. "The poor," in other words, can too easily think that it is *they,* not *"the rich,"* that count for more in God's eyes.

Some observers, like the 19th century philosopher, Friedrich Nietzsche, thought that this, in fact, was the whole purpose behind Christianity. In referring to it as a "slave morality," Nietzsche's point is that it serves, and was always meant to serve, the psychological and emotional interests of the poor masses, namely their interest in exacting a sort of imaginary vengeance against the wealthy by demonizing them while insisting upon their own "blessedness."

Admittedly, Nietzsche was an enemy of Christianity. But he *became* an enemy *after* having been raised Christian by his Lutheran minister father. In any event, one needn't accept Nietzsche's reading of Christianity—I do not—in order to see that those Christian leaders who use their pulpits to blast "inequality" lend it considerable plausibility.

Finally, Jesus excoriated "the rich," yes; but He was no less hard on "the poor," including and particularly His closest followers. Conversely, sometimes Jesus lavished praise upon "the rich."

For 2,000 years, whether rightly or wrongly, Christendom's worst villain has been, not the rich and famous Herod, Pilate, or Nero, but Judas Iscariot, one of Jesus' closest disciples and a "poor" man who relinquished what possessions he may have had in order to follow Him. Moreover, Jesus regularly castigated his "poor" disciples for their lack of faith, and, sometimes, compared them unfavorably with wealthy Gentiles, like the Roman Centurion whose *servant* Jesus healed.

Moreover, it is worth noting that besides Himself, the greatest example of Christian charity that Jesus extolled is that of the Good Samaritan, a *rich* man who deployed some of his ample resources to help a stranger in need.

We also shouldn't forget that Nicodemus and Joseph of Arimathea were rich members of the priestly class with whom Jesus must've been particularly close, for not only did they attempt to prevail upon their fellow Pharisees to refrain from turning Jesus over to the Romans. Following Jesus' crucifixion, both prepared His body for burial in the tomb that Joseph secured for Him.

All of this can be found easily enough in the four canonical Gospels which are read in Christian churches throughout the world every Sunday. That these points are neglected by so many ministers is due, I submit, to their obsession with combating, not poverty, but "inequalities" in income and wealth—a topic, this Christian has been at pains to show, having nothing to do with either the whole of the Bible or The New Testament.

Christianity and Its Critics

The world's largest religious tradition has had more than its share of critics over the centuries. A not inconsiderable number of these have been men and women (but mostly men) of genius. And the brightest and most constructive of critics have tended to be Christ's own disciples.

That popular funny man and political leftist Bill Maher, along with his millions of fans, think that this low brow comedian deserves to be included among the ranks of Christianity's ablest objectors is a tragic commentary on the condition of our culture's collective intellect.

The saddest thing about all of this—and I see it regularly among my college students—is that most people who either explicitly reject Christianity or refuse to treat it with the utmost seriousness that it warrants *do not have a clue as to what it is.*

Christianity looks ridiculous only after it has been made to look ridiculous. In other words, High priests of the popular culture, pseudo-intellectuals like Maher, cheat: they attack, not Christianity itself, but a one-dimensional, cartoonish caricature of it. Socrates would have likened Maher and his ilk to shadow boxers who prefer to swing at the air rather than contend with a real opponent.

Considering that at no time or place has there ever existed an intellectual tradition as rich and complex as that of Christianity, we should expect nothing less—and nothing more—from lightweights like Maher. If they didn't have *straw men* they would have nothing.

But it isn't just uneducated troglodytes like Maher who style themselves worthy adversaries of the Christian faith. Such public intellectuals as the late Christopher Hitchens, Sam Harris, and Richard Dawkins have also jockeyed for this distinction—but to no avail.

Despite the popular acclaim with which the intelligentsia greeted them, the critiques of Harris and Dawkins are indebted to a worldview that is as antiquated as Christianity appears to be to them. Though both men are scientists, the problem lies not in their science, but in their *scientism.* The latter is the doctrine that all claims to knowledge can and should be brought before the tribunal of "the scientific method." Those claims and only those claims that satisfy this absolute criterion constitute genuine knowledge.

Scientism collapses the variety of human voices into one voice, the voice of science or pseudo-science.

But scientism, in turn, is a species of Rationalism, an intellectual orientation that reached its zenith during the Enlightenment.

In other words, the ideas of Harris and Dawkins, far from reflecting some ideal of objective (and timeless) truth, are in reality a function of the prejudices—indeed, the myths—of an age.

Hitchens is no better.

Though neither a scientist nor a proponent of scientism, this arrogant Englishman was as ignorant as Harris and Dawkins of the fact that the assumptions on which his atheistic critique of Christianity rests bear the unmistakable impress of his generation. Moreover, the content of his critique consists of the recycling of arguments that had been thrown up against Christianity for centuries—but by men whose minds were far more discriminate than that of his own.

There exist intelligent objections against Christianity. But they come largely (if not exclusively) from its adherents. This is a paradox but it is true. As Saint Augustine famously said: "Believe in order to understand." Only those who are thoroughly immersed in a practice or tradition know all of its nuances. It is only they who know it inside and out.

Hence, it is only Christians, when they are intellectually curious and honest, who can at once identify the challenges that their religion faces *and* meet those challenges.

The "new" atheists mentioned here are as competent to adequately critique, much less undermine, Christianity—or *any* religion, for that matter—as is a person who has never been married eligible to do the same with respect to marriage.

Jack Kerwick

No Political "Progressivism" in the Christian Past

In the Western world today, particularly in America, there persists this idea among both Christians and non-Christians alike that, to be a Christian, one must endorse a specific kind of vision of how societies should be organized politically.

While it is true that few if any contemporary Christians endorse a theocracy, and while it is true that few advocate on behalf of anything approximating a utopian politics, it is no less true that a good number, and possibly most, Western Christians are political *perfectionists*.

In political philosophy, perfectionism is an approach that assigns to the state or government the role of cultivating virtue in its citizens. Not unlike any and every theory, perfectionism admits of multiple variations. But common to all of its versions is the belief that government has a positive educative function, the belief that government is supposed to be an agent of character formation.

Communism and socialism are forms of perfectionism, certainly, but so too are the theories of Aristotle, Thomas Aquinas, and any number of other approaches that needn't have much else in common with such modern collectivist ideologies.

When Pope Francis (and legions of other Christians) demand of the governments of affluent Western societies that they admit into their countries potentially limitless numbers of immigrants and refugees from alien cultures, and they make this demand, whether explicitly or implicitly, in the name of Christ, they betray a commitment to Christian perfectionism. After all, it is only the peoples of European lands, i.e. those whose ancestors were historically Christian and who built the most affluent societies the world has ever known, at whom the Pope and his ilk aim their moral imperatives.

Christianity and the World

Christianity requires, Francis would have us think, for the governments of the West—or, more precisely, the taxpayers who subsidize them—to make a range of provisions for the millions of strangers entering their lands, regardless of the costs.

When Christians, on the alleged basis of their religion, maintain that the United States government must finance and defend Israel; provide "foreign aid;" abolish capital punishment; criminalize suicide, prostitution, and recreational drug use; make the world safe for Democracy; and, comprehensively, serve the world in being a City on a Hill, they reveal their perfectionism.

Things were not always so.

Jesus Himself said simply: "Give to Caesar what belongs to Caesar, and give to God what belongs to God."

St. Paul was clearly no perfectionist. Admittedly, after his encounter with Christ on the road to Damascus, the man formerly known as Saul was interested in nothing other than spreading the Gospel to the Gentile world. Paul was a brilliant theologian, a scholar of the Hebrew Scriptures (The Old Testament), and, most importantly, an apostle. He spent little time writing about politics. Yet from what he did say we can abstract the bare outlines of a certain kind of vision of politics.

Paul wrote: "Let every person be subject to the governing authorities; for there is no authority except from God, and those authorities that exist have been instituted by God." The state is "God's servant" ordained, not to make citizens into good and pious individuals, but to instill "terror" through "the sword" in those who act criminally. None are to resist the authorities, Paul says, for the latter derive their authority from God and exist for the sake of making society a tolerable, peaceful place to live. "Do you wish to have no fear of the authority? Then do what is good, and you will receive its approval; for it is God's servant for your good. But if you do what is wrong, you should be afraid, for the authority does not bear the sword in vain! It is the servant of God to execute wrath on the wrongdoer" (Romans 13: 1-4).

St. Augustine (354-430) is perhaps the most influential Christian thinker of all time and one of the most influential philosophers, Christian or otherwise. A bishop, prolific writer, and master rhetorician, Augustine brought his prodigious intellectual powers to bear upon the formation of a Christian *philosophy*, something that heretofore didn't actually exist. More specifically, Augustine was the first Christian thinker to treat, philosophically, the subjects of time, history, motion, eternity, and creation. His contributions have proven to be immeasurable.

In political philosophy, Augustine pursued the direction in which Paul pointed. There are two "cities," he said, "the earthly city" and "the city of God." These are not literal, geographical regions but spiritual and moral conditions. Those who are of the earthly city live according to "the flesh." Conversely, those who are of the city of God live according to "the spirit."

Each city is distinguished from the other on account of what it loves. Those of the earthly city are driven by "the love of self, even to the contempt of God," while the inhabitants of the city of God are motivated by "the love of God, even to the contempt of self."

Even so, the earthly city "has its good in this world, and rejoices in it with such joy as things can afford." The end of the earthly city is peace, "well-ordered concord of civic obedience and rule," "the combination of men's wills to attain the things which are helpful to this life." Peace, even a temporal peace of the sort for the sake of which the earthly city exists, is a good.

However, this peace "is rather the solace of our misery than the positive enjoyment of felicity." The state is supposed to essentially constrain vice, not promote virtue.

Ultimately, though, there is no true justice in this world, for true justice is to be found only "in that republic whose founder and ruler is Christ [.]" And what this in turn implies is that "kingdoms" are "but great robberies" and "robberies themselves" are "but little kingdoms."

At this time when "progressivism" has infiltrated Christian denominations in the West, it would behoove Christians to acquaint themselves with their tradition.

The Challenges of Purism and Atheism to Christianity

While 2 billion people—one third of the Earth's population—celebrate the Birth of all births at this time of year, Christmas—or at least the conventional manner of celebrating it—remains an object of derision, even of contempt, for some.

For all of their differences, its discontents—unbelievers, non-believers, and Christian "purists" alike—unite in mocking it for the pagan symbols that have come to be associated with it.

Given that their self-assuredness is as invincible as is their condescension, the discontents would have us think that Christians are unaware of the pagan sources of many of their Christmas-oriented traditions. Not only is this not the case; Christians are the people who originally appropriated what the pagan world had to offer in order to enrich their celebrations of Christmas.

And there isn't anything in the least objectionable about this—at least not from a Christian perspective.

Christmas marks the birth of Christ, i.e. the event whereby God assumed *flesh*: the Incarnation. God, you see, transcends the world, yes, but He is also immanent in it.

Christianity, in other words, precludes those species of purism that insist that there is some allegedly "original" Christianity that can be separated out, neat and tidy, from the paganism new and old that have corrupted it. There is no such thing. God's Word is as dynamic, as lively, as creation itself. Indeed, creation *is* as much God's word as is the Bible, reason, and tradition.

In becoming "all things to all people," as he described himself, St. Paul's belief in this truth was second to none. Those Christians who conscripted aspects of the pagan world into the service of developing both their theology as well as their worldview have done exactly what the greatest of Apostles, Paul, did when he brought the Gospel to the gentile world.

Christian purists should consider that charging the contemporary celebration of Christmas with lacking in authenticity for its pagan influences is like charging as inauthentic any version of the Bible that isn't written in Hebrew or Greek. Atheists and nonbelievers should consider that this allegation is akin to the charge that modern science is inauthentic or hypocritical because of *its* origins in Christianity.

And make no mistakes about it, science has emerged and flourished in the West precisely because of the religion of the West. More specifically, Christianity relies upon metaphysical assumptions that are, or have always been, absent from much of the world.

First, for Christians, the world does not, as the ancient Greeks supposed, *emanate* from a deity. And, unlike what Easterners of various sorts assumed, the world is neither an *illusion* nor identical with an abstract, impersonal "Absolute" or *Tao*.

Rather, the universe is a *creation,* an entirely, fundamentally distinct thing from the Supremely Personal, all benevolent, omniscient Being that made it. Because of its divine origins, it is purposeful, meaningful, and *good*. The universe, then, is an object that both can and should be studied. Thus, Sir Isaac Newton, one of the founders of modern science, spoke for legions of some of history's most renowned scientists—Galileo, Kepler, Boyle, to name but a few—when he famously remarked that in doing science, the scientist was doing nothing more or less than "thinking God's thoughts after Him."

So too is what we call "morality" indebted to Christianity. If Christmas is a fake because popular celebrations of it have their roots in a pre-Christian world, then morality as Westerners conceive it is as well a fake because of *its* roots in Christianity.

There are two notions central to Western morality—"secular" morality—that are *distinctly* Christian. It's their combination that is *uniquely* Christian. The first is that all human beings, regardless of their individuating characteristics—"race, color, creed," etc.—possess an inviolable dignity, a worth beyond all price for having been created by an all perfect, all loving God. The second is that each of us has an obligation to *act* toward each person as we would act in the presence of God Himself, for in the presence of each person, we *are* in the presence of God.

And to fulfill this obligation the God-Man—Christ—gave us the example of His own Person. To treat others as if we were serving God is to care, genuinely *care*, for them, and to do so at once tirelessly *and* joyfully.

That Christ's disciples fail to fulfill their calling, that they've *sinned,* they are the first to admit. As their Lord taught them through His own self-sacrificial life, humility is a cardinal Christian virtue. Still, given the foregoing considerations, to say nothing of the fact that the overwhelming majority—*the overwhelming majority*—of the planet's charitable organizations are Christian-based, no one with two eyes to see who isn't a boldfaced liar could so much as think to deny that Christianity has been as powerful an engine for good as any to which the world has ever given rise.

In the interest of keeping this engine humming along, decent people everywhere should, with one voice, shout "Merry Christmas!" this Christmas season.

Christianity and the Crusades

It's a sad commentary on our time that *anyone,* to say nothing of the President of the United States of America, would so much as *think*, much less publicly announce, that there is some sort of moral equivalence between the contemporary phenomenon of Islamic barbarity and such oft-cited examples of Western and American injustices as the Crusades, slavery, and Jim Crow. Some comments are in order.

First, critics who make the "That Was Then, This Is Now," argument against Obama not only sorely miss the point; they actually *legitimize* his contention that Christians *are* guilty of the charge that Obama levels against them.

The truth is that while *individual* Crusaders, like individual soldiers in every war, were indeed guilty of some horrible things, the Crusades *as such* were just. Obama typifies the Christophobe who can't resist treating the Crusades as an axiomatic instance of Christian villainy while conveniently refusing to mention that they were a response to *centuries* of *Islamic* aggression.

That's right: For *centuries* Islamic armies had been *conquering* Christian lands generally and the Holy Land specifically. And the invasion into Europe was well underway by the time Urban II issued a call for the first holy war in 1095.

"From the confines of Jerusalem and from the city of Constantinople," the Pope exclaimed, "a grievous report has gone forth [.]" The word was indeed "grievous," for "a race from the kingdom of Persians," what the Pope characterized as "an accursed race," "has violently invaded the lands" of Christians "and has depopulated them by pillage and fire."

These Persians—Muslims—"have led away a part of the captives into their own country, and a part," he says, "they have killed by cruel tortures." Churches had been destroyed and "the kingdom of the Greeks" has been "dismembered" and "deprived of territory so vast in extent that it could not be traversed in two months' time."

Obama is right that the Crusades most certainly were conducted by Christians in the name of Christ. But unless defending one's person and property against those who mean to deprive one of them is immoral, the Crusades *per se* amounted to an eminently just enterprise. That abuses and even atrocities occurred in the Crusades no more establishes the injustice of the Crusades *as such* than does the fact that abuses, and even atrocities, occur within marriages and families establish the immorality of marriage and family *as such*.

Second, slavery had been a global institution from time out of mind. In the Christian world, and in America, slavery was not conducted "in the name of Christ," as Obama maintains. It's true that slave owners, including and especially *Christian* slave owners, frequently alluded to the Bible to show that the *fanatical* abolitionists' charge that slavery was a *sin* was unsustainable. However, many of these same Christian slave holders nevertheless believed that slavery *was* an evil that needed to be abolished.

Even still, only a woefully impoverished moral imagination could fail to recognize the relevant differences between, on the one hand, the situation of slavery in which earlier generations of Americans found themselves, to say nothing of the situation of Jim Crow (!) that Americans eradicated more recently, and, on the other, the situation that ISIS and other Islamic jihadists are creating for their victims whenever and wherever they rear their beastly heads. Indeed, such is the sophomoric character of Obama's moral vision that it would be laughable if it weren't so damn offensive—and dangerous: In one and the same breath, he speaks of *both* a white segregationist's refusal to associate with blacks *and* an Islamic fanatic's refusal to grant mercy to a person who he instead cages and eventually *burns to death*.

Third, more galling than Obama's historical illiteracy and moral idiocy is his rank hypocrisy. Though he talks of "we" when implying moral parity between Islamic violence and the violence perpetrated by Christians in the past, Obama most certainly does *not* mean what he says. What he is *really* saying is that *you*—all of you *white Christians*—must not shed any of that *white guilt* that's paid off so well for the Barack Obamas of the world.

Let's be frank: Leftists like Obama have been able to perpetuate the fiction—the invidious fiction—that, to paraphrase one of his fellow leftists, the white race is "the cancer" of the planet, by ignoring the evils committed by the world's peoples of color. For you see, when the historical conduct of whites is compared with, not contemporary Western standards, but the historical—and *present*—conduct of *all* peoples, it becomes crystal clear that the injustices for which whites, and white Christians in particular, are forever being blamed and for which they are forever atoning are common to the human species.

But more than this, remarkably, it is only among whites, and especially among white Christians, that a genuine moral revulsion of these perennial practices arose. Whites, especially white Christians, though the majority and the wielders of power in the West, made enormous sacrifices to rectify not just those wrongs that were done to *fellow white Christians;* but as well those wrongs suffered by *non-whites and non-Christians*, both in the West and *beyond*.

Obama and his ilk in the Racism-Industrial-Complex have too much to lose if this dirty little secret gets out.

It is this, more so than anything else, that explains why, in the light of the Islamic savagery on display in the fatal burning of a Jordanian pilot, Obama *had* to warn us against getting on "*our* high horse."

Christianity and "Fundamentalism"

I had an interesting experience recently that has got me to thinking about a topic that is all too rarely addressed by practicing Christians.

Not long ago I decided to obtain a Facebook account. One of my "friends" is someone to whom I haven't spoken in nearly 20 years, a woman—"Andrea," I will call her—who I knew when I was a kid. As it turns out, this virtual "friendship" was as long for this world as whatever friendship we had as children, for shortly after offering an abrupt response to one of my characteristically philosophical/theological posts, she deleted me from her "friends" list.

It would be an exercise in futility to disclose the specific details of our exchange; suffice it to say that Andrea, being a self-professed disciple of Christ, evidently believes that questions of the sort that I, as a philosophy professor *and* a Christian, make my living exploring, are not only unimportant but offensive, if not *blasphemous*. Neither philosophy nor *religion* has any bearing on a person's relationship with God. All that is needed is Jesus, she adamantly insisted.

That Jesus is "the Way, the Truth, and the Life," is a proposition with which I wholeheartedly agree; but that faith in Christ should somehow preclude the need or desire for reflective thought—what I take Andrea was insinuating—is patently absurd on its face.

If this single incident were an isolated phenomenon, it wouldn't be worth remarking upon. Yet it is anything but that. The Andreas of America—who I will call, for lack of a better term, "Christian Fundamentalists"—are legion, and they are virtually to a man and woman solidly ensconced on "the right." Because of this, it is the rare "conservative" publication that dares to address them. It is for the sake of rectifying this that I write this column.

All too seldom noted are the striking similarities between the Christian Fundamentalist (just Fundamentalist from now on) and the left-wing Rationalist. Most importantly, while the latter's contempt for tradition has long been observed, what has gone unnoticed is that the former's contempt might just be at least as great. Though the leftist seeks to "deconstruct" our traditions, he at least has to engage them in order to accomplish his objective. The Fundamentalist, though, disregards them altogether.

Fundamentalism, as I am using that term, transcends denominational lines, but it is particularly salient within Protestantism. "*Sola scriptura*"—Scripture alone—is, after all, a Protestant principle. Whatever its historical nuances, taken to its extreme conclusion, the logic of the concept has rendered the Bible an idol. However, *this* false god is even more transcendent than the One True God, for the latter, Christians have always professed, though transcendent, is also *immanent*, and at no time has He been more so than when He became a Man.

But the idolatry of the Fundamentalist leads him or her to deny that the world—culture, history, tradition, i.e., *human intelligence*—has anything at all to do with the composition of Sacred Scripture or the development of the doctrines that we read in it. Ready-made, it presumably dropped from the heavens, the one and only "key" whereby the answer to every conceivable question can be unlocked by anyone and everyone who will but avail himself of it.

Andrea's comment to me is as straightforward an illustration of this view as any that I have encountered—and I have had many such encounters. In rejecting all intellectual inquiry as worthless, she derides an infinitely rich complex of intellectual, ethical, and spiritual traditions—in a word, Western civilization—that were millennia in the making. We can only thank God that Christians haven't always thought as Andrea thinks.

Contrary to what the Fundamentalist believes, what we today call "the Bible" was centuries in the making. Not only were its "books" composed under varying circumstances by various authors, but there was rigorous, heated debate for centuries more after Christ as to what scriptures are "sacred" and, thus, deserving of being incorporated into "the canon." The Scriptures that were eventually settled upon were preserved throughout history due to the tireless work of the relatively few literate men—monks primarily—who translated and copied them by hand. Had these Christians from generations of long ago adopted the attitude of my former "friend" toward intellectual endeavor, it would have been quite some time since Christianity would have run aground.

Yet the Christianity that Andrea and other Fundamentalists purport to champion is an invaluable inheritance that God has chosen to bequeath to us not just through the authors of the Bible, but through a staggering array of men (and some women) of genius and vision: artists, philosophers, theologians, mystics, scientists, and other thinkers: Saint Augustine and Saint Thomas Aquinas; John Duns Scotus and William of Ockam; Michelangelo; DaVinci; Newton; Galileo; Dante; Shakespeare; Milton; Chaucer; Beethoven; Handel; and many more too numerous to recount here.

The world in which we live, Western civilization, if it existed at all, would be radically unlike anything that Westerners had ever known if not for the priceless contributions of Christians over the last 2,000 years.

So, to my former friend and "friend," and to the countless others who share her view, I can only say that while I agree with them that, ultimately, Jesus is all that is "needed," they would be well served to consider that Jesus is as "Incarnate" today as He was two millennia ago. Only today He is incarnate, not in a physical body, but in the world, in hearts and in minds, in intelligence, passion, conviction, and every other good which God makes available to the human race.

A "Jesus" who is located exclusively between the two covers of a book, who "lives" only through select Biblical quotations that have been divested of all context and who is resurrected by his self-appointed guardians to beat down those who *they* deem to be insufficiently holy is a lord alright, but he is as far from *the Lord* as we can get.

Jack Kerwick

Christianity and Stephen Hawking: Amateur Philosopher Syndrome (APS)

There can be no question that Stephen Hawking is a brilliant scientist.

But he is a lousy philosopher, and an even worse theologian.

If ever it was in question, Hawking's speech at Caltech last week established beyond doubt that the world-renowned physicist suffers from Amateur Philosopher Syndrome (APS).

Scientists, particularly popular scientists, like Hawking, are especially prone to APS. All such scientists see the world, not so much scienti*fically,* as scient*istically.* That is, they assume that there is but one legitimate tongue in which to speak of reality: the language of science. All others are dismissed.

Three aspects of Hawking's lecture reveal his to be a classic textbook case of APS.

First, while referring to this as a "glorious time" in which we have succeeded in coming "this close to an understanding of the laws governing us and our universe," Hawking referred to human beings as but "*mere* collections of fundamental particles of nature" (emphasis added)[.]

Second, as The Daily Mail reported on Thursday, Hawking mocked "the religious position" on the origins of the universe by likening it to "the myth of an African tribe whose God vomited the Sun, Moon, and stars."

Finally, Hawking assured his audience that, thanks to "general relativity" and "quantum theory," we can now account for the origins of the universe without any appeals to God at all: our universe, like one foamy bubble among countless others, might just be one of an infinite number of other universes.

Christianity and the World

To the first point, the question must be posed: From whence springs the assumption that we are "*mere*" combinations of physical particles? There are at least two problems with a scientist using the word "mere."

The first is that "mere" is an evaluative, not a descriptive, a philosophical, not a scientific, term. As Hawking uses it, is likely intended as a *meta*physical—not a *physical*—word. It suggests *insignificance*. But, scientifically speaking, it is as inappropriate to speak of the significance or insignificance of the world as it is to speak of its beauty and ugliness, or its sweetness and bitterness. These are not attributes of the universe; they are attributes of *our minds* that we *project* onto the world.

The second problem is that "mere" is exhaustive. To say that X is "merely" this or that is to say that it is *only* this or that. Science—real science, not philosophical or ideological dogma masquerading as science—can't speak to ultimate questions. That's the job of philosophy and theology. Science can determine that we are bundles of material particles, but it most definitely cannot determine whether we are merely this.

What stuns most of all is just how illiterate in the philosophical and theological traditions of Western civilization Hawking appears. For millennia, Jews and (later) Christians have found the idea of God "vomiting" the universe to be just as primitive, just as crass, as it strikes Hawking as being. The reason for this is not hard to grasp: if God puked up the universe, then He didn't *create* it. Rather, the world flows out of God, or from pre-existing stuff.

Jews are unique in world history in being the first to affirm the existence of one supreme God who *created* the world *out of nothing*.

This is crucial, for it is this belief that the world is distinct from, yet created in the image of, an all-good and all-wise being, from which the scientific enterprise was born. As long as the world is thought of as a distinct creation of God, it is assumed to be both rational and good, i.e. a proper object of study.

In short, neither science nor the scientist Stephen Hawking ever would have arisen had it not been for this conception of divine creation that Hawking ridicules without having grasped.

There is one last point that bears mentioning.

The notion of a sea of "universes" that Hawking invokes is both logically troublesome and theologically irrelevant. The word "universe" is a synonym for "everything." So, claiming that there is an infinite number of "universes" makes about as much sense as claiming that there is an infinite number of "everythings."

But even if there is some sense to be had from the idea of multiple universes, and even if these universes have always existed, this doesn't for a moment circumvent the fundamental question: Why is there something rather than nothing? *This* is what we want to know when we ask about the beginning of the universe.

And, contrary to Hawking, explaining the existence of a universe by referring back, and only back, to the universe itself is like accounting for one's own existence by looking no further than oneself.

The verdict: Hawking hasn't come close to showing that we can dispense with the God hypothesis in explaining the presence of the universe.

Christianity and Stephen Hawking: Amateur Philosopher's Syndrome (APS) II

Last week, world-renowned physicist Stephen Hawking addressed legions of enthusiastic students and others at Caltech. According to reports, the gist of his speech was that "general relativity" and

Christianity and the World

"quantum theory" can enable us to account for the origins of the universe *without* positing the existence of God.

According to The Daily Mail, Hawking ridiculed the religious position on this topic by likening it to the myth of an obscure African tribe whose God "vomited the Sun, Moon, and stars." He further mocked the traditional theistic explanation of the world's beginnings by referring back to an exchange that Martin Luther is said to have had with a younger man who ventured to discover what God was doing "before" He decided to create the universe. "Was he preparing Hell for people who asked such questions?" "Such questions," Hawking maintained, are nonsense.

As Christians have noted for the better part of 2,000 years, they are indeed nonsensical. Hawking would have known this had he, say, read St. Augustine's *Confessions*—a Western classic that supplies us with an analysis of time that secular and religious thinkers alike acknowledge remains unrivaled for its insights. Yet this is the problem: Hawking, not unlike most scientists who have made a splash in the popular culture, seems to be almost scandalously ignorant of the philosophical and theological literature that defines his civilization.

Augustine conceded long ago that the question, "What was God doing before He created the world?" is fundamentally misplaced. He knew what Hawking now knows: the world did not come to be *in time*, but, rather, time is an aspect or dimension of the world. Thus, since "before" is a temporal word, there was no "before" God created the world, for there was no time until God created it.

As far as the idea of God puking up the universe is concerned, Christians (along with Jews and Muslims, for that matter) have always found this as primitive and repugnant a conception as does Hawking. Again, it is shameful that he apparently doesn't know this, for it is elementary.

Unlike, say, Hindus and ancient Greeks, Christians staunchly deny that the universe "emanated" from God, or that God brought it into being from some "stuff" that already existed. And, of course, they just as stanchly deny that God is a physical being, a body. Yet this is all that is implied in Hawking's metaphor of the god of his African tribe.

For the Christian, the world is not contemporaneous with God, the way a person is contemporaneous with his shadow, say, or the bile in his stomach. Rather, God is the Supreme Being, immaterial and, thus, invisible, who created the world *out of nothing*.

In fact, ironically, it is precisely because of the belief that the world is the product of an all-good God that science has soared to such heights as it has. In the absence of this Christian doctrine, it is much more likely than not that science itself would have been absent from the West. It is the idea that the material cosmos, by virtue of being the handiwork of the Perfect Architect, is both real and good that the universe was deemed an eminently worthwhile object of investigation.

If not for this "religious position," there would have been no science—and no Stephen Hawking.

There is a final point. As Christian (and other) thinkers have noted for centuries and centuries, the universe is not self-explanatory. Hawking might agree, which is why, I think, he has theorized that our universe is but one universe among an infinite number of such universes. But this line only pushes the problem back a step.

First, since "the universe" is but a short-hand term for everything or all things, to speak of infinite universes is like speaking of infinite everythings, or limitless all things. Neither logically nor grammatically does it seem to make much sense.

However, the bigger obstacle to Hawking's view is philosophical or theological. Let's just suppose that there is more than one universe. So what? The basic question over which atheists and theists have been clashing from time immemorial is: Why is there something rather than nothing?

Hawking never states the question this directly—and for good reason.

Whether there is one universe or an infinite number of universes, nothing composed of parts—as the universe is—is self-explanatory. In other words, to explain the universe or universes, we must go *beyond* them.

Why is X here? Unfortunately, for the Hawkings of the world, it is logically illicit to answer this by pointing to X itself.

Hawking may be a great scientist, but he is a lousy philosopher—and an even worse theologian.

The Christian Subtext to "Secular" Christmas Classic Films

That there is some sense in which Christmas can be said to have become "secularized" over the years is undoubtedly true. Nevertheless, this judgment may be overwrought. Perhaps Christ is more present in "secularized" expressions of Christmas than either Christian or non-Christian is willing to acknowledge.

This is borne out by close examination of such "secular" Christmas cinematic classics as *A Christmas Carol, It's a Wonderful Life,* and *Miracle on 34th Street.*

"Christmas" literally means "the Mass of Christ." Thus, though often unintended, each and every use (and misuse) of the word "Christmas" throughout the season references the Christ. The decorations and lights; department store sales; songs; "holiday" film and television programs; the practices of gift-giving and exchanging cards; "holiday" work parties; school concerts; family dinners and gatherings—there would be none of it if not for the carpenter from Nazareth.

Even Santa Claus—jolly ol' Saint Nicholas—took flight from the life of a Godly fourth century Catholic bishop.

There would be no Christmas if not for Christ. And because the former is as ubiquitous as it is, particularly in the Western world, every Christmas season renders it impossible for anyone to be entirely ignorant of "the Reason for the Season."

Or maybe it is accurate to say that just as God the Son became *incarnate* in human flesh, so too does He become incarnate in every manifestation, every sign, of the Christmas season.

What I am here arguing is that there is a closer connection between *the* Miracle, the Birth of Jesus, and the "miracles" commonly associated with it in popular depictions of Christmas than has been acknowledged.

Dickens' *A Christmas Carol,* for example, never explicitly mentions Christ. There is nothing overtly Christian in the idea of ghosts or spirits haunting a wretched man on Christmas Eve. At the same time, it is not coincidental that of the 365 days and multiple holidays from which Dickens could have chosen to make the backdrop of his tale, he chose *this* day and *this* holiday.

Ebenezer Scrooge is an old man who, in the early morning hours of the day that the Christian world reserves to celebrate the birth of God, discovers the reasons for the despair to which he long ago succumbed. Courtesy of his encounter with its "spirits," Scrooge experiences the miracle of Christmas as he undergoes a radical conversion, a rebirth of the spirit reminiscent of that which Saul of Tarsus had to endure on the road to Damascus before he could become Paul, God's ambassador to the Gentiles.

Those who lose their lives will save them, Jesus insisted. To achieve the supreme good, genuine, eternal happiness, one must die to oneself and be reborn in Christ. This death occurs when the heart, like an empty shell that has been dropped on concrete, shatters. Christians call this contrition. It's what Scrooge suffered on Christmas Eve.

Christianity and the World

Recognizing his vices for what they were—selfishness, greed, pride, bitterness, mercilessness—Scrooge, with the help of some supernatural beings, slayed his old self. By dawn of Christmas morning, he was born again, a new creation committed to living a life of charity in the most Christian sense of this term. "Charity," some may forget, derives from the Latin "caritas." In Christian theology, caritas became synonymous with (the Greek) "agape," the unconditional love for others.

By way of the miracle of Christmas, Scrooge transformed from near-spiritual death into a man consumed with a passion for loving others as he loves himself.

It's a Wonderful Life is another popular Christmas film with a Christian subtext. Jimmy Stewart's character of George Bailey is a good, but frustrated, man. For all of his life, George has deferred pursuing his lofty dreams for the sake of fulfilling his duties, or what he took to be his duties, to his family, friends, and local community of Bedford Falls. On Christmas Eve, his frustration gives way to despondency as George—in covering for his absent-minded uncle who misplaced the family business's proceeds long enough for the film's villain, the Scrooge-like Mr. Potter, to steal it—finds himself facing prison time. But as he is about to hurl himself from a bridge into the cold running river below, an angel, Clarence, intercedes.

When George tells Clarence that the world would have been better had he never been born, Clarence decides to prove him wrong by revealing to George an alternate reality that is George Bailey-free. Through much pain, even horror, George discovers that the life that he just a short time earlier regretted was actually quite...wonderful.

George Bailey is a character to which average folks, Christians especially, can readily relate. He not only harms no one; George is good to others. Still, he has not yet crucified his old self. In fact, despite his modest circumstances—or is it *because* of these circumstances?—George isn't just *in* the world. He obviously is very much *of* it.

He resents that he never left his hometown.

He resents the Bailey Savings and Loan Bank that his father built and that, from George's perspective, has prevented him from achieving his dreams.

He resents that he doesn't have as much in the way of material goods as some others.

In a particularly unguarded moment, George even expresses resentment that he has *children,* the family that he evidently views as but another hindrance to the life that he wanted for himself.

But through the miracle of Christmas, George, like Scrooge, has his sight restored. Scrooge was a bad man that became good. George was a good man who became a better man. Both, though, were *surprised by joy,* as C.S. Lewis memorably titled one of his books. Via the miracle of Christmas, both underwent a miraculous transformation when they discovered the secret to joyful living: *gratitude.*

Both George and Scrooge recognized existence generally and their personal lives specifically as *given,* i.e. as *gifts* for which to be thankful. Yet if thanks are due, then they must be owed to some*one*. In the instances of George Bailey and Ebenezer Scrooge, it's clear that it is someone greater than themselves to whom their gratitude belongs.

And, to repeat, both came to this realization by way of supernatural assistance at Christmas.

Miracle on 34th Street, though regularly characterized as a "secular" holiday film, bears upon it the unmistakable impress of Christianity. For starters, as is abundantly clear by the title, this movie centers around what it portrays as a miracle of sorts. Secondly, the latter occurs at—when else?—Christmas.

An elderly man by the name of "Kris Kringle" arrives at the Macy's Thanksgiving Day parade claiming to be the *real* Santa Claus ("Kris Kringle", recall, derives from the German

"Christkindl," meaning "Christ Child."). He is the embodiment of kindness and cheeriness. Kris is in the world, but not of it, for the world that he wishes to change is marked by a crass "commercialism," as he describes it. This is a world (eerily similar to that in which we find ourselves) that exploits Christmas for the purposes of profit, status, greed. It is a world that has forgotten not just the true meaning of Christmas. It has abandoned all sense of vision, moral imagination. The world of *Miracle* assigns negative value to anything that can't be readily reduced to an instrument for some immediately practical use or other.

The world that Kris enters is signified by Doris Walker (Maureen O' Hara), her seven year-old daughter, Susan (Natalie Wood), and Macy's psychiatrist, Dr. Granville Sawyer (Porter Hall). Doris, a single mother, is a decent but jaded woman who thinks that being "truthful" with her daughter means forbidding her from believing in "fairy tales, like Santa Claus." Sawyer, in contrast, is the penultimate symbol of all against which Kris rails: mean, contemptible dishonest. The goodness exemplified by Kris and his young friend Alfred, a teenage employee of Macy's who enjoys dressing up as Santa and distributing presents to children at the YMCA, Sawyer writes off as a function of mental illness.

As His contemporaries sought to remove the Prince of Peace from their world by nailing Him to a cross, so too does the world, represented by Sawyer, seek to remove Kris by way of a sort of social death: Sawyer attempts to have him institutionalized in a mental hospital.

Goodness, though, ultimately prevails. An idealistic lawyer, Fred Gailey (John Payne), quits the prestigious legal firm for which he works in order to prove to the world that Kris Kringle *is* Santa Claus. Just as Christ was considered "foolishness to the Gentiles," as St. Paul puts it, Kris was considered the same by the self-appointed guardians of the world around him. But just as Christ radically subverted the epistemic hierarchy of the world, so too does Kris, via Fred, do the same.

Sawyer is disgraced and terminated. Doris begins to soften her heart and, along with Susan, begins to believe in Kris. She allows herself to love and be loved by Fred. The world is redeemed. Hope dawns anew.

And this miraculous chain of events occurs, not incidentally, during the season of Christmas.

Marriage, Logic, and Religious Liberty

So-called "same sex marriage" is the issue of the week. The Supreme Court is expected to make a ruling on its constitutionality in the month of June.

My prediction: "same-sex marriage" will soon become the law of the land.

My reason for this is simple: Conservatives who claim to favor "traditional marriage," "disbelieve" in "same sex marriage," and oppose "the redefining" of marriage have ceded too much ground to their opponents.

And they have ceded this ground by speaking of *traditional* marriage (as if there was any other kind), their *belief* that marriage is between a man and a woman (as if this was a question of belief), and their opposition to the act of *redefining* marriage (as if it was within anyone's power to define or redefine marriage).

In short, by way of their arguments (or *non*-arguments) against "same sex marriage," conservatives actually reinforce the idea—long championed on the left—that institutions are "social constructs," artifacts that government, or "society," can create and destroy at will.

The problem with this reasoning is that if institutions, like marriage, really have been arbitrarily constructed by government, then there is no reason that they shouldn't be *de*constructed in the event that Equality or some other ideal demands this course.

Christianity and the World

With an eye toward ascending from the mire of confusion in which far too many of us have been wading for far too long, I offer the following comments.

First, homosexuality may be the most moral, most natural, most divine-like activity in which human beings are capable of engaging. No matter. The fact remains that marriage can no more accommodate homosexuals than bachelorhood can accommodate those who are married.

Just as bachelorhood is a state of being that inherently excludes the married, so too is marriage a state of being that inherently excludes homosexuals. Thus, the language of "same sex marriage" is as self-contradictory, as ridiculous, as that of "married bachelorhood."

To put it another way, "same sex marriage" is no marriage at all.

Inseparable from this first point is another: This issue is not now, nor has it ever been, about "the redefinition" of marriage. It is as impossible for you or I or the Supreme Court to redefine marriage as it would be for any of us to redefine bachelorhood.

Human beings invent words, it is true, but our words are pointers, vehicles by which we express and relay concepts or ideas. This is crucial, for internal to each idea is its own logic that makes it the idea that it is. So, for example, whatever word we choose to affix to the concept of a bachelor, the concept of a bachelor has always been and will always be the concept of an unmarried man.

Even if there are no bachelors, even if we somehow managed to drop the word "bachelor" from our vocabulary, never to use it again, the logic of the concept once denoted by this word would remain forever in tact: a bachelor could never be anything other than an unmarried man.

The case is much the same with the concept of marriage. The government can choose to allow homosexual unions and endow them with the term "marriage." And, in theory, the government can allow married people to regard themselves as "bachelors." In reality, however, the government can no more allow "same sex marriage" or "married bachelorhood" than it can decree that the world started yesterday.

Third, as points one and two make clear, it makes about as much sense to say that one "believes" that marriage is between a man and a woman as it does to say that one "believes" that only single men should be considered bachelors. Marriage is what it is, an essentially heterosexual union. It is not an object of *belief*; it is an object of *knowledge*.

Finally, the supporters of "traditional marriage" must stop their talk of "traditional marriage." Besides lending legitimacy to the proposition that there *are* forms of marriage other than the heterosexual variety, the term "traditional marriage" is meaningless by reason of redundancy. There is no *traditional* marriage. There is only marriage.

Like I said, these considerations aside, in all likelihood the government will eventually ascribe the label of "marriage" to those homosexuals who want for their unions to be recognized as such. An ever growing number of people fail to see why anyone would or should have a problem with this. But there *is* a problem.

Every change, however great or small, is purchased at a cost. The loss of the familiar and the uncertainty regarding the new situation produced by a change are costs common to all changes. Because of this, the prudent have always preferred changes that are small and gradual to those that are grand and transformative.

Yet the kind of change in our marital arrangements that the Supreme Court is presently contemplating is a change of the latter kind: never in the history of the world has anything like it been conceived, much less seriously considered. Only fools and liars would have us believe that there won't be a substantial price to be paid for legalizing "same sex marriage."

Admittedly, I don't think that marriage will suffer as a consequence of this. Marriage is far more threatened by a hypersexualized popular culture, the ease with which divorces are pursued and granted, etc. Still, while marriage may be no worse off as a result of the legalization of "same sex marriage," our liberty just may be.

American liberty consists of all of the liberties laid out in our Constitution. If any one of these liberties is threatened, the entire system is imperiled. Now, freedom of religion is a fundamental liberty. If it becomes unconstitutional to prevent homosexuals from "marrying" other homosexuals, then religious organizations that refuse to accommodate homosexuals along these lines may very well become convicted of acting unconstitutionally. Hence, freedom of religion, along with freedom of conscience, will be forever lost.

This is anything but a far-fetched scenario. Consider that the vast majority of the proponents of "same-sex marriage," and virtually all of its most militant supporters, are located solidly on the left. Then consider that for at least a couple of centuries, leftist revolutionaries and radicals have recognized religion to be the most formidable obstacle to their designs, for the religious insist upon deferring to an authority higher than that of the government.

What better way to weaken religion than to coerce its practitioners to submit to the state? And what better way to coerce its practitioners than by threatening them with, not only legal penalties, but the threat of acting disreputably?

Thoughtful people, regardless of their religious, political, or sexual orientations, will realize that the issue of "same sex marriage" is not just, and not even primarily, about marriage.

Judaism, Christianity, and Morality

There is much talk these days about something called "*Judaeo-Christian values.*" This is the name that is invariably assigned to the *morality* to which America is supposed to have traditionally subscribed. America, we are told, is a "Judaeo-Christian" nation, a nation "founded" upon "Judaeo-Christian *principles*" or "*ideals*."

Now, it is, of course, true that there is an especially close relationship between Judaism and Christianity. The latter spun out of the former. The first Christians were Jews, and the Man who the Christian world—approximately one-third of the planet's population—recognizes as God Almighty was *a Jew*. To those writings that Jews regard as sacred Christians attach the same importance. In fact, though he doesn't often think of himself in exactly these terms, if pushed, the Christian would be the first to acknowledge that he is indeed a Jew, but a *perfected* Jew, a Jew who lived to witness the coming of the Messiah—*the Christ*.

Yet for all of these similarities, the expression "Judaeo-Christian morality" is, ultimately, a fiction that does an injustice to both Judaism and Christianity.

The "values," "principles," or "ideals" encompassed by "Judaeo-Christian morality" are to the traditions from which they have been abstracted what a portrait is to the whole life of the person of whom it is a depiction. The values, principles, and ideals of "Judaeo-Christian morality" stand in relation to the faiths from which they've been distilled as the principles of a grammar stand in relation to the living language to which they belong. Just as a portrait and a grammar derive their value from their usefulness in summarizing the vastly more intricate phenomena to which they owe their being, so too are "the principles" of any morality nothing more or less than bloodless, lifeless abstractions, static abridgements of the living tradition of which they are cliff notes.

Strictly speaking, neither Judaism nor Christianity is a "morality" at all. Both are *religions*. It is true that from these religions we can extract principles, values, and ideals. It is even true that we can, with some justice, gather them up and label them "morality." But what we *cannot* do is think of them *solely* in terms of morality, or think that this label is anything other than a term of convenience, a term with all of the short-hand value and literal truth as the expression, "the sun rises." The sun does not literally rise. Nor can it literally be said that Judaism and Christianity are "systems" of morality.

The principles, ideals, and values of Judaism and Christianity are intelligible only because of the unmistakably *theological* context within which they take their place. In short, if we insist on speaking of Judaism and Christianity as "systems" at all, we should be clear that they are systems, not of morality, but of religion. Their principles assume meaning only because they are carefully situated within a narrative of which no less a being than God Himself is at the center. It is for the purpose of shaping themselves into the kind of person who will love self, neighbor, and God *for God's sake* that their adherents are expected to observe "the principles," affirm "the values," and pursue "the ideals" of these two great religious traditions.

Once these principles, ideals, and values become disembodied, as it were, once they are boiled down into a doctrine of "natural rights," say, or some fixed set of principles alleged to be "self-evident" or "innate" or demanded by "human nature" or "Reason," they lose their identity and, with it, their power to inspire and motivate.

Now, the concept of "Judaeo-Christian" morality is even more of a distortion than the concepts of "Jewish *morality*" and "Christian *morality*." Judaism and Christianity are both religious traditions, but there is a very real respect in which we can say that they affirm different deities.

With a few exceptions here and there, Christians the world over essentially agree on the *triune* nature of God. That is, in stark contrast to Jews, Christians believe that God is Three Divine Persons—God the Father, God the Son, and God the Holy Spirit. To Jewish ears, this doctrine of the Blessed Trinity can only smack of the worst of sins, the sin of *idolatry,* for to non-Christians of all faiths it appears to be an affirmation of *polytheism*. And Judaism is noted for nothing if not its fierce monotheism.

Christianity, of course, is *not* a version of polytheism. It is as monotheistic as Judaism. But Christians have arrived at their peculiar conception of God because of another that they embrace, one in the absence of which Christianity would not be the religion that it is. From this doctrine Jews and other theists recoil in sheer horror. It is called the Incarnation. Inasmuch as it embodies the conviction that, not *this* or *that* "god," but the one and only *God* of all that is, from sheer love, chose to became *a human being*, it is truly unique.

Yet this isn't all.

It isn't just that God became a man. According to the story of the Incarnation, God became a man who, for the sake of the human race, both bore unimaginable *suffering* as well as the most humiliating of *deaths*. To put it mildly, the God of Christianity strikes non-Christians as insufficiently transcendental. To put it more bluntly, such a God comes across as scandalously immanent.

But the God of Christianity *is* the Person of Jesus of Nazareth.

The God that Christians worship entered human history and, as the prologue to John's Gospel states, "dwelt among us." Like that of any other human being, Jesus' identity was the product of the historical and cultural circumstances in which He lived. This He appears to have known better than anyone, for in order to thrust His significance upon His contemporaries, Jesus carefully—masterfully—weaved His image from the various threads of His own Jewish tradition.

Unlike, say, Muhammad, who gathered together a series of allegedly divinely inspired orders and commands devoid of any narrative framework, Jesus saw to it that His life, or at least His public ministry, was nothing less than a dramatic reenactment of the collective self-understanding of His (Jewish) people. Yet it was also something more than this, for in *reenacting the past,* He also *revised* popular conceptions of it. And in doing the latter, there is a real sense in which He *recreated the present* and *re-envisioned possibilities for the future.*

Jesus is what in another idiom we may describe as a "moral exemplar." For Christians, it would be said that he is a moral exemplar *par excellence*. Here is a man who *immersed* Himself in the tradition within which He was born and reared. Jesus wasn't content in achieving mere *fluency* in His tradition; He successfully sought *connoisseurship* in it.

Jesus made no ringing affirmations of such abstract notions as "human dignity," "rational nature," "personhood," and "human nature," much less "self-evident" "human rights." He knew that human flourishing could occur only within the concrete context of tradition—His tradition, the *theological* tradition of Judaism. It was this tradition that Jesus sought to reshape and fulfill in His own Person, but ultimately in His passion, death, and resurrection from the dead.

For Christians, then, "morality" is not essentially, or even primarily, a matter of observing "principles," pursuing abstract ideals (like Equality or Justice), or following rules and commands. "Morality" consists in the emulation of a person, or a Person. Jesus is indeed *the* exemplar of stellar conduct for Christians. But the conduct in question is not, strictly speaking, moral conduct; it is *godly* conduct.

Christians (and Jews) aspire toward godliness. The religious are concerned with *religiosity,* not "morality."

"Morality," especially when it is a morality of abstract universal "principles" and "ideals," is "the desiccated relic," as one philosopher once put it, the residual fragments, of a tradition.

More specifically, it is, at least in the West, the traces of a religious tradition.

Jack Kerwick

A Religious or Politically "Progressive" Papal Encyclical?

Laudato Si', Pope Francis' latest encyclical, is quite provocative. Unfortunately, though, it provokes us to consider the possibility that its author has more in common with contemporary leftism than traditional Christianity.

The Pope's encyclical read as essentially nothing more or less than a protracted, theologized, reiteration of the same "progressive" drivel that's been drooled upon us for decades.

For example, Francis writes: "A very solid scientific *consensus* indicates that we are presently witnessing a *disturbing warming* of the climatic system" (emphasis added).

Notice, the Pope manages to pack into this one sentence talking points that are part and parcel of the rhetorical arsenal from which his secular counterparts routinely draw: Not only do *all*, or at least *most,* scientists agree ("consensus") that global warming is a reality; they agree that this phenomenon is something ominous, something that is "disturbing."

And, of course, while conceding that "there are other factors" that could account for this danger, Francis concurs with his secular ideological counterparts in claiming that "a number of scientific studies indicate that most global warming in recent decades" is "due...mainly" to "human activity."

Fundamentally, from beginning to end, the agreement between Francis and those at home sounding the clarion call on "climate change" is total. "Climate change," His Holiness continues, "represents one of the principal challenges facing humanity in our day."

Observe: Among the gravest of problems to which this Pope devotes an entire encyclical is not the unspeakable acts of brutality to which scores of Christian men, women, and children are daily subjected by Islamic militants in countries throughout the Third

Christianity and the World

World, or even the oppression of Christians in such affluent lands as America who are now confronted with legal penalties for failing to violate the dictates of their own consciences by funding abortion services for their employees or accommodating gay wedding celebrations.

It is climate change that holds this distinction.

Francis, predictably, exempts the world's poor of responsibility for climate change. It is on the shoulders of—who else?—*Westerners* that he lays the lion's share of blame. "Many of those who possess more resources and economic or political power seem mostly to be concerned with masking the problems or concealing their symptoms [.]"

In short, we in the West are guilty not only of creating most of this "disturbing warming;" we are guilty as well of evading responsibility for our crime.

By "wasting water," both Westerners and, to a lesser extent, those in "developing countries" deny the poorest of the world's poor their "right to life" and "their inalienable dignity." Access to clean drinking water, you see, is "a basic and universal human right, since it is essential to human survival and, as such, is a condition for the exercise of other such rights."

Here is another respect in which Francis reveals his leftist proclivities: Rights, he maintains, are *entitlements* to *substantive* satisfactions, to *resources*. Thus, if I am thirsty but haven't any money to procure a drink, I am entitled to *your* services just and only insofar as you are able to satiate my thirst. Relieving my thirst now becomes your *duty*. In failing to fulfill this "duty," you are now guilty of violating my "right to life" and my "inalienable dignity."

We can take this logic further. Shelter, presumably, must be "a basic and universal human right" too, for "it is essential to human survival" as well. What this implies is that if you and your family are without shelter, and I have even the slightest room in my home where I live with my family, then regardless of the costs for me that this may entail, I have a duty to accommodate you and yours.

You are *entitled* to nothing less.

When speaking of the poor's "inalienable right" to water, the Pope says as much when he speaks of the "grave social debt" that we owe them. And he follows through on the logic of the "positive rights" to which he speaks when he goes on to claim that we can fulfill this debt, at least partially, by way of "an *increase in funding*" (emphasis added).

But it gets worse.

Francis insinuates that funding can only go so far as long as there remains "little awareness of the seriousness of such behavior"—wastefulness—"within a context of great inequality."

Read carefully: Ultimately, it isn't "climate change" or "global warming" that the encyclical is about. It is *inequality,* "*great* inequality," that is the evil that is the center of attention.

And notice how the Pope implies that in perpetuating or even allowing inequality—again, inequality of *resources*—we are guilty of violating the *right to life* of those who have less than us.

Now, it has always been understood that to violate a person's right to *life* is to *unjustly kill* that person. Yet if an unequal "distribution" (another word that Francis is fond of using) of resources is such that it impedes the poor's access to goods that are essential to existence, then, according to the Pope, the poor's "right to life" is undermined. But if this is so, then it is those of us who have freer access to these goods, those of us who have permitted this inequality to persist, who are guilty of violating the poor's "right to life."

We are, then, in effect, *murderers.*

A lot more can be said about *Laudato Si'*. But the one thing that we *cannot* say about it is that it has anything to do with the Gospel of Christ.

Christianity and the World

Planned Parenthood: Is Abortion Immoral or Not?

As many (but not enough) people now know, for quite some time, Planned Parenthood has been designing their abortion services for purposes of harvesting and selling the organs of the human beings that they routinely kill.

It would appear that this has gotten folks from across the political divide pretty upset.

But the outrage raises questions.

Either abortion is morally reprehensible or it is not. If it is reprehensible, then it is so presumably because abortion is the unjustified killing of an innocent, defenseless human being. The fate of the *corpse* is either of no moral relevance or, at the very least, of far less moral significance than the fact that a corpse was *produced* to begin with.

If abortion is not morally reprehensible, then the fate of the aborted human being that's been separated from its mother should no more concern us than should the fate of a wart, cyst, tumor, or a skin tag that's been removed from a patient concern us.

In both cases, the shock and indignation expressed by both Republicans and Democrats, "conservatives" and "liberals," to the latest revelations regarding Planned Parenthood are morally confused.

Some Republicans, like presidential contender and Kentucky senator, Rand Paul, now advocate on behalf of defunding Planned Parenthood. They *now* call for this. Indeed, Planned Parenthood most definitely should be deprived of government monies. It's a disgrace that taxpayers were ever forced to subsidize it.

But if Planned Parenthood should be defunded, it is because it has been routinely slaughtering the most vulnerable human beings for decades. Do Senator Paul and his cronies mean to suggest that it is only because of what Planned Parenthood does *after* it has killed a human that it deserves to be denied government funds? And since everyone has known that this organization has been killing human beings for years and years, are not Paul and his colleagues now implying that it is permissible to fund abortion services, as long as the corpses are disposed of, rather than harvested?

The Republicans' demand to defund Planned Parenthood is the right one. Yet given their timing, this sounds more like politics and less—much less—like sound, moral reasoning.

Of course, those Democrats, like Hillary Clinton, that now claim to be "disturbed" or "concerned" about this Planned Parenthood scandal also sound disingenuous.

The Democratic Party has been America's official "pro-choice" party since the early 1970's. According to the party line, mothers are morally entitled to kill their offspring—as long as their posterity remains in their wombs. This has been Democrats' position, a position that they have spared no measure in defending.

Of course, Democrats never frame their view in quite these terms: They defend not "mothers'" rights, but "*women's*" rights. And it certainly isn't a right to "kill their offspring" that Democrats advocate, but the right to "*choose,*" or the right to "*abort the pregnancy.*"

All talk of a child or baby or even a human being is conspicuously—intentionally—absent from the vocabulary of the proponents of "choice." Instead, there is the "fetus."

Are we now expected to believe that these same Democrats are bothered to discover that agents of Planned Parenthood are selling the body parts of "aborted" "fetuses?"

Democrats can't even bring themselves to refer to abortion as a form of killing at all. Thus, they insist upon speaking—and have been remarkably successful in convincing others to speak—of "*abortion.*" There is and can be no talk of "*killing,*" lest it become suspected that the object of abortion is human.

But this being so, on what grounds could any proponent of "choice" be troubled by the trading in body parts that's occurring at Planned Parenthood?

No one should be surprised that those who support the killing of human beings in the womb would be unperturbed by using their *remains* for ostensibly noble purposes—or any purposes: If it is permissible to extinguish "fetuses'" lives, then why should it matter, morally, what one does with the dead?

But neither should those who regard as a moral evil the killing of human beings in the womb be all that troubled by the purposes to which their *remains* are put, for the grave moral evil here *is* the killing of human beings in the womb.

Again, either abortion is immoral or it is not. In terms of moral relevance, whatever happens *after* the abortion comes in a distant second to the abortion—if it even registers at all.

Will the Real Jesus Please Stand Up?

Who is Jesus?

Upon reading the Scriptures, it becomes clear that the *real* Jesus, as opposed to the tamed, lame, and *maimed* Politically Correct Jesus who Christian clerics as much as anyone have been promoting for years, was the antithesis of the meek, mild mannered, nonjudgmental man of whom Christians and non-Christians alike hear about at every turn. The latter placates this generation's political-moral sensibilities, but he hardly fits the profile of a person who gave rise to a religion claiming billions of followers.

The truth about Jesus, in His own day as in ours, is hard.

For starters, "Marcionism" was a school of thought from the second century that distinguished the God of the Old Testament from the God of the New. Though it was recognized early on for the heresy that it is, to hear many contemporary Christians, including and especially clergy, one could be forgiven for thinking that Marcionism is Christian orthodoxy.

Though God in the Old Testament repeatedly reveals His love for and patience with His people, He just as often proves that this love is not at all incompatible with bloodshed and death. In fact, judging from the Hebrew Scriptures, divine love—which is inseparable from the divine justice—not infrequently *demands* punishment.

In other words, the God who flooded the Earth and ordered the Israelites to slaughter every living thing among their neighbors *is* the babe who was born in a manger to a humble young virgin.

However, even "the God of the *New* Testament," i.e. Jesus, was most definitely anything but meek and mild. Meek and mild human beings tend not to draw huge followings of fans that are willing to sacrifice their very lives for them. They tend not to polarize whole populations, command the attention of the most powerful leaders and rulers, and get themselves executed as capital offenders against the largest empire the world had ever seen (up to that point).

Jesus was neither meek nor mild by the standards of His own day. By the lights of the self-appointed guardians of secular liberal orthodoxy—both Democrats *and* Republicans, "liberals" *and* "conservatives"—He is nothing less than scandalous: Jesus, to the politically respectable, can only be judged a "hater," a "fear monger," a "bigot," and maybe even a "sexist!"

After all, Jesus had the audacity to refer to a poor Canaanite woman who begged for Him to heal her daughter as a "dog." "It is not fair to take the children's food and throw it to the dogs," Jesus sternly informed her. It was only after the woman persisted—"Yes, Lord, yet even the dogs eat the crumbs that fall from their masters' table"—that Jesus relented and healed her little girl (Mathew 15: 21-28).

Christianity and the World

As for judging, Jesus spared no occasion to remind both fans and foes alike that He and "the God of the Old Testament" *are* one and the same:

"So it will be at the end of the age. The angels will come out and separate the evil from the righteous and throw them into the furnace of fire, where there will be weeping and gnashing of teeth" (Mt. 13: 49-50).

"Whoever is not with me is against me…but whoever speaks against the Holy Spirit will not be forgiven, either in this age or in the age to come" (Mt. 12: 30-32; Mk. 3:19-30; Lk. 11:14-23).

For His enemies, the Pharisees and scribes, Jesus reserved a furry of criticism. They were "hypocrites," "blind guides," "whitewashed tombs" who are "full of the bones of the dead and of all kinds of filth" like "greed and self-indulgence." His opponents are "descendants of those who murdered the prophets," "snakes" and "vipers" who can't "escape being sentenced to hell" (Mt. 23: 16-36; Mk. 12: 38-40; Lk. 20: 45-47) [.]

Yet even those who styled themselves His friends didn't escape His wrath.

Unfaithful servants will be "cut" into "pieces" and placed "with the hypocrites, where there will be weeping and gnashing of teeth" (Mt. 24:51; Lk. 12: 41-48). Jesus informs His disciples of His plans for those *nations* with which He is displeased: "Then he [the Son of Man] will say to those at his left hand, 'You that are accursed, depart from me into the eternal fire prepared for the devil and his angels…And these will go away into eternal punishment" (Mt. 25: 41-46).

Of the cities of Chorazin, Bethsaida, and Capernaum, Jesus likened them to the cities of Tyre, Sidon, and Sodom—cities to which He (God) laid waste. "But I tell you [Chorazin and Bethsaida], on the day of judgment it will be more tolerable for Tyre and Sidon than for you. And you, Capernaum…you will be brought down to Hades" (Mt. 11: 22-23; Lk. 10: 13-15).

Jack Kerwick

"If any of you put a stumbling block before one of these little ones who believe in me, it would be better for you if a great millstone were fastened around your neck and you were drowned in the depth of the sea" (Mt. 18: 6; Mk. 9:42-48; Lk. 17: 1-2).

If Jesus were on the Earth with us right now, PETA would've long ago made Him into Public Enemy Number One, for Jesus, upon curing a man of demons, sent the demons into a herd of about 2,000 pigs, propelling the swine down a hill into a body of water in which they drowned. Not only, though, did legions of defenseless animals die; the livelihoods of people who depended upon these animals were also destroyed. "Then they [the townspeople} began to beg Jesus to leave their neighborhood" (Mt. 8:28-9:1; Mk. 5:1-20; Lk. 8:26-39).

I could continue.

Some other details about the real Jesus that we never hear:

While Jesus did indeed show great love to the poor and powerless, He also showed great love to the rich and powerful. Joseph of Arimathea and Nicodemus were wealthy and influential members of the Sanhedrin—and disciples of Jesus. The Centurion whose servant Jesus healed was, obviously, a man of means—and of power.

And, of course, God the Son, as the Christian's Old Testament readily reveals, always extended blessings to such super wealthy and powerful rulers—and *kings* to boot!—as King David and King Solomon, etc.

Though He condemned *some* rich people, He also condemned *some* poor people. And, contrary to the narrative that the socialist-minded clerics of today have labored tirelessly to ensconce in the popular consciousness, it wasn't *only* the rich and powerful that conspired to execute Jesus; *the poor,* many of the very folks to whose needs He attended with great care, turned on Him in *His* hour of need and demanded—*demanded!*—His death: According to all four Gospels, when given the choice to spare the life of

Christ or that of the murderous zealot, Barrabas, the bloodthirsty crowd of mostly poor folks chose the latter.

Jesus was no pacifist: At least some of His disciples were armed with swords, and at one juncture, Jesus even *commands* His disciples to arm themselves. "And the one who has no sword must sell his cloak and buy one," He ordered them (Lk. 22: 36). All four Gospels inform us of how Jesus burst upon the Temple in Jerusalem and cleared house by flipping over the tables of the traders and driving them and their animals out with a whip!

Jesus also used military imagery in His parables, and heeded a Centurion's request (without admonishing him, as He admonished so many others—like Levi, the tax collector—to repent of *his* ways). Furthermore, the martyrology of the early church included soldiers).

To serve Jesus, we must first know Him from the idol—the false god—with which "polite society" has replaced Him.

WORKS CITED:

CHAPTER I: Christianity and the Transformation of History

1. Kennedy, D. James. "What if Jesus Had Never Been Born?" *Imprimis* 24 (1995). https://imprimis.hillsdale.edu/what-if-jesus-had-never-been-born/ (accessed July 13, 2017)
2. Stark, Rodney. *The Rise of Christianity: A Sociologist Reconsiders History*. Princeton: Princeton University Press, 1996. 97.
3. Ibid. 97-98.
4. Ibid. 97.
5. Ibid. 102.
6. Ibid. 104.
7. Ibid. 104-105.
8. Esolen, Anthony. *Politically Incorrect Guide to Western Civilization*. New York: Regnery, 2008. 116.
9. D'Souza, Dinesh. *What's So Great About Christianity?* New York: Regnery Faith, 2008. 69-70.
10. Esolen, Anthony. *Politically Incorrect Guide to Western Civilization*. New York: Regnery, 2008. 40.
11. The Thomas Coram Church of England School http://www.thomascoram.herts.sch.uk/thomas-coram/ (accessed July 13, 2017)
12. *American Experience: Frontline*. "God in America: A New Eden" http://www.pbs.org/godinamerica/transcripts/hour-two.html (accessed July 13, 2017)
13. Graham, Ruth. "What American Nuns Built." *Boston Globe*, February 24, 2013. https://www.bostonglobe.com/ideas/2013/02/24/what-american-nuns-built-what-american-nuns-built/IvaMKcoK8a4jDb9lqiVOrI/story.html_(accessed July 13, 2007)
14. Thorne, Ashley, "US Founding Fathers on Education: In their own Words," *National Association of Scholars* (2010). https://www.nas.org/articles/u_s_founding_fathers_on_edu

cation_in_their_own_words (accessed July 13, 2017)
15. Mercer, Ilana. "Trade in Voodoo for Values." *World Net Daily*, Jan 21, 2010. http://www.wnd.com/2010/01/122714/ (accessed July 13, 2017)
16. D. James Kennedy. "What if Jesus Had Never Been Born?" *Imprimis* 24 (1995).
17. Esolen, Anthony. *Politically Incorrect Guide to Western Civilization*. New York: Regnery, 2008. 57.
18. D'Souza, Dinesh. *What's So Great About Christianity?* New York: Regnery Faith, 2008. 68.
19. Ibid. 75.
20. Wikipedia: History of Hospitals. https://en.wikipedia.org/wiki/History_of_hospitals (accessed July 17, 2017)
21. For more, see Jonsen, Albert. *A Short History of Medical Ethics*. Oxford: Oxford University Press, Reprint edition 2008.
22. Quoted in C. Ben Mitchell, "The Christian Origins of Hospitals," *Bible Mesh Blog*, February 6, 2012. https://biblemesh.com/blog/the-christian-origins-of-hospitals/ (accessed July 17, 2017)
23. Rosenberg, Charles E. *The Care of Strangers: The Rise of America's Hospital System*. Baltimore: John Hopkins University Press, 1995.
24. D'Souza, Dinesh. *What's So Great About Christianity?* New York: Regnery Faith, 2008. 65.
25. Kennedy, D. James. "What if Jesus Had Never Been Born?" *Imprimis* 24 (1995). https://imprimis.hillsdale.edu/what-if-jesus-had-never-been-born/ (accessed July 17, 2017)
26. Stark, Rodney. *The Victory of Reason: How Christianity Led to Freedom, Capitalism, and Western Success*. New York: Random House, 2005. 52-53.
27. Ibid. 52.
28. Ibid. 51.
29. McGrath, Alister. *Christianity: An Introduction*. 3rd ed. Oxford: Wiley, 2015. 273.
30. Stark, Rodney. *The Victory of Reason: How Christianity Led to Freedom, Capitalism, and Western Success*. New York: Random

House, 2005. 30.
31. See Eric Metaxas', *Amazing Grace: William Wilberforce and the Heroic Campaign to End Slavery*. New York: HarperOne, 2007.
32. See Thomas Sowell's, *Race and Culture: A Worldview*. New York: Basic Books, 1995.
33. Stark, Rodney. *The Victory of Reason: How Christianity Led to Freedom, Capitalism, and Western Success*. New York: Random House, 2005. 24.
34. For an analysis of individuality in ancient Confucian thought, see Huston Smith's, *The World's Religions: Our Great Wisdom Traditions*. Revised edition. New York: HarperOne. 1991.
35. Novak, Michael. *On Two Wings: Humble Faith and Common Sense at the American Founding*. New York: Encounter Books, 2002. 6-7.
36. Ibid. 7.
37. Ibid. 8, emphases original.
38. Ibid. 8-9, emphases original.
39. Ibid. 9.
40. Stark, Rodney. *The Victory of Reason: How Christianity Led to Freedom, Capitalism, and Western Success*. New York: Random House, 2005. 12.
41. Ibid. xi.
42. Ibid. 12.
43. Ibid. xi, emphasis added.
44. Ibid. 12, emphases original.
45. Ibid. 13.
46. Ibid. 14.
47. Quoted in Ibid. 14-15.
48. Ibid. 22.
49. Ibid. 63.
50. Ibid. 56.
51. Ibid. 58.
52. Ibid. 61-62.
53. Ibid. 62.
54. Reed, Fred, "The Place of Christianity in History: A View from Without," *Fred on Everything*, April 27, 2017.
https://fredoneverything.org/the-place-of-christianity-in-history-

a-view-from-without/ (accessed July 17, 2017)

CHAPTER II: Christianity and Morality: The Atheist's Problem of Moral Goodness

1. Harris, Sam. *Letter to a Christian Nation.* New York: First Vintage Books, 2008. 7-8.
2. Ibid. 8
3. Ibid. 25.
4. Ibid. 24.
5. Ibid. 23-24.
6. Ibid. 24.
7. Ibid. 21.
8. Ibid. 22.
9. Nietzsche, Friedrich. *On the Genealogy of Morals.* Trans. Horace B. Samuel. New York: Barnes and Noble, 2006. 12.
10. Ibid. 156.
11. Ibid. 155.
12. Sartre, Jean-Paul. *Existentialism is a Humanism.* Trans. Carol Macomber. New Haven: Yale University Press, 2007. 27.
13. Ibid. 28.
14. Ibid. 29
15. Ibid. 21
16. Ibid. 22
17. Ibid. 29
18. Mackie, J.L. *Ethics: Inventing Right and Wrong.* Reprint. London: Penguin, 1990. 45.
19. Ibid. 15.
20. Ibid. 16.
21. Ibid. 16-17
22. Ibid. 17
23. Ibid. 41
24. Ibid. 42
25. L.A. Selby-Bigge, Hume, David. *A Treatise Concerning Human*

Nature. 2nd ed. eds. P.H. Nidditch and L.A. Selby-Bigge. Oxford: Oxford University Press, 1978. 466-467.
26. Ibid. 467-468
27. Ibid. 468-469
28. Ibid. 469
29. Kant, Immanuel. *Critique of Practical Reason*. New York: Garland, 1976. 225.
30. Ibid. 226.
31. Ibid. 228
32. Ibid. 232
33. Ibid. 228.
34. George Mavrodes, "Religion and the Queerness of Morality," in *Rationality, Religious Belief, and Moral Commitment*, eds. Robert Audi and William J. Wainwright. Ithaca: Cornell University, 1986. 215-216.
35. Ibid. 217.

CHAPTER III: The Rational Defensibility of Christianity vs. Atheism's Weak Case Against It

1. *St. Anselm's Basic Writings*. 20th ed. trans. S.N. Deane. Chicago: Open Court, 1996.
2. Dawkins, Richard. *The God Delusion*. Boston: Mariner, 2006. 104.
3. Ibid. 105.
4. For a fuller discussion of Hume's philosophy and his critique of ontological argument, see, Hume, David. *Treatise on Human Nature*. ed. Ernest C. Mossner. New York: Penguin, 1969; and Hume's *Dialogues Concerning Natural Religion* in *David Hume: Writings on Religion*. ed. Antony Flew. Chicago: Open Court, 1992.
5. *The Summa Theologica of St. Thomas Aquinas, 5 vs.* trans. Dominican Fathers of English Province. New York: Benzinger Bros., Inc., 1947.

6. See *Diderot Encyclopedia: The Complete Illustrations. 5 vs.* trans. Roger Lewinter. New York: Harry N. Abrams, 1978.
7. Leibniz, Gottfried. *New Essays on Human Understanding,* 2nd ed. trans. and ed. Jonathan Bennett and Peter Remnant. New York: Cambridge University Press, 1996.
8. Kant, Immanuel. *Critique of Pure Reason.* ed. and trans. Paul Guyer and Allen Wood. New York: Cambridge University Press, 1999.
9. Oppy, Graham. *Ontological Arguments and Belief in God.* New York: Cambridge University Press, 2007. 145.
10. Russell, Bertrand. *Why I am not a Christian.* London: Watts, 1927.
11. Quoted in Dawkins, Richard. *The God Delusion.* Boston: Mariner, 2006. 107.
12. Malcolm, Norman. "Anselm's Ontological Arguments." *The Philosophical Review* 69 (1960).
13. Aquinas, Thomas. *Summa Theologica,* Part I, trans. Dominican Fathers of English Province. New York: Benzinger Bros., Inc., 1947.
14. Dawkins, Richard. *The God Delusion.* Boston: Mariner, 2006. 101.
15. See Avicenna. *The Metaphysics of the Healing.* Trans. Michael E. Marmura. Chicago: University of Chicago Press, 2005.
16. See *Ockham: Philosophical Writings: A Selection.* Revised ed. transl. Philotheus Boehner. Cambridge: Hackett Publishing, 1990.
17. Frederick Coppleston's famed BBC debate with Bertrand Russell as recorded in Russell's, *Why I am not a Christian.* London: Watts, 1927.
18. This argument of Hume's can be found in his *Dialogues Concerning Natural Religion,* Part IX (1779).
19. Kreeft, Peter and Ronald K. Tacelli. *Handbook of Christian Apologetics: Hundred of Answers to Crucial Questions.* Downers Grove: Intervarsity Press, 1994. 54.
20. Ibid. 54-55
21. Flew, Antony. *There is a God: How the World's Most Notorious Atheist Changed His Mind.* New York: Harper Collins, 2009.

96.
22. Ibid. 97
23. Ibid. 99
24. Ibid. 99-100
25. Ibid. 75
26. Quoted in Ibid. 76-7